"The last couple of years have seen an explosion in AI technology, and, more importantly, the accessibility of this technology via a smartphone has the potential to drive an enormous impact. Sales and marketing are both an art form and a science. The demands and expectations of the modern buyer continue to drive the need for ever-increasing sophistication. Marrying together the needs of a modern sales and marketing team with the power of AI makes *Let AI Be Your Coach* an essential guide for sales and marketing professionals and leadership."

—CHRISTOPHER PENNINGTON, senior vice president of global sales, EcoVadis

"AI's intersection with the layperson's work and life has evolved from the mysterious to the novel—'something to be feared' that seemed to appear overnight with a ChatGPT launch and would displace all work in a year became an alternative search tool that conversed in natural language or a way to enhance a portrait and 'smooth the lines' to something more complimentary and friendly.

Today, AI is collaborating with humans in ways that give us leverage. Many are finding that using AI tools allows us to spend more time doing what we enjoy and what we are good at. Sales reps spend more time talking to relevant prospects and less time prospecting. Marketers tailor a more personalized, relevant message to each segment of their audience. Small businesses spend more time catering to their customers and less time doing what they are not great at but know they must do, like marketing and administration. Executives make more informed decisions and help their teams get leverage, scale, and compete with organizations they may not have historically been able to compete with.

In *Let AI Be Your Coach*, Shashank assembles the guidance everyone will need to stay relevant and connected in a changing world where AI, when put to good use, will be a natural part of personal development and growth. This book will help readers take the first or next step toward creating a better life for themselves by integrating AI in a natural way, offering a guide on how to use AI so you can focus on, develop, and showcase your unique strengths."

—**FRANK J. VELLA**, CEO, Constant Contact

"For most professionals, there is a gap between the hope of what's possible with AI platforms and the reality of how we can actually leverage it for our businesses. Shashank's book, *Let AI Be Your Coach*, provides a practical bridge over this gap. It allows leaders to see real-world examples of how AI can be leveraged to empower teams, improve customer experience, and grow revenue."

—**MELISSA LANGDALE**, founder and CEO, Praxis Lending Solutions

"This book gets AI right—as a coach, not a crutch. It's clear, practical, and grounded in real operating experience. Shashank offers a thoughtful, actionable guide for sales and marketing leaders who want to apply AI with discipline and intent, not just talk about it."

—**GIRI DEVANUR**, founder and executive chairman, reAlpha

"There's a lot of noise around AI and *Let AI Be Your Coach* cuts through it. Shashank treats AI the way high performers actually should, as a thinking partner and a performance coach. It's practical, grounded, and refreshingly honest. If you want to use AI to genuinely improve how you work, this is a must-read."

—**CHRIS SMITH**, author of the international bestseller *The Conversion Code*

LET AI BE YOUR COACH

Unlocking Transformation and Mastery for Sales and Marketing

SHASHANK SHEKHAR

AN INC. ORIGINAL

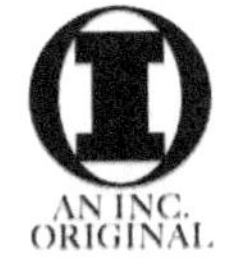

An Inc. Original
New York, New York
www.anincoriginal.com

This work is being published under the An Inc. Original imprint by an exclusive arrangement with Inc. Magazine. Inc. Magazine and the Inc. logo are registered trademarks of Mansueto Ventures, LLC. The An Inc. Original logo is a wholly owned trademark of Mansueto Ventures, LLC.

Distributed by River Grove Books

Design and composition by Greenleaf Book Group
Cover design by Greenleaf Book Group
Cover image used under licence from © Adobe Stock/master1305

Publisher's Cataloging-in-Publication data is available.

Print ISBN: 978-1-63909-069-3

eBook ISBN: 978-1-63909-070-9

First Edition

Contents

Introduction—Practical AI: A Playbook for Real Results 1

PART 1—THE AI COACHING REVOLUTION

1. The AI Advantage: Transforming Organizations
   from the Inside Out 9

2. From Chaos to Clarity: Building an AI-Powered
   Knowledge Base 35

3. AI: The Ultimate Strategist, Mentor, and Coach 53

**PART 2—COACHING IN SALES:
HOW AI TRANSFORMS SALES PROFESSIONALS**

4. AI, The Ultimate Rainmaker: Supercharging
   Prospecting and Lead Generation 65

5. From Rookie to Rock Star: AI-Driven Sales Role-Playing . . 81

6. AI in the Driver's Seat: Turning Data into
   Smarter Sales Moves 99

**PART 3—COACHING IN MARKETING: AI'S ROLE IN
CREATIVE STRATEGY AND CAMPAIGN SUCCESS**

7. Marketing's New Muse: AI-Powered
   Creativity and Strategy 121

8. Launch, Learn, Optimize: How AI Makes
   Your Marketing Smarter 149

9. One to Millions: How AI Personalizes Marketing
   Like Never Before. 179

PART 4—BUILDING SKILLS AND LONG-TERM SUCCESS WITH AI COACHING

10. The AI Accelerator: Fast-Tracking Skills and Mastery . . . 203

11. From Wishful Thinking to Winning:
AI-Powered Goal Mastery 225

PART 5—THE FUTURE

12. The Rise of Agentic AI: From Theory to Practice 249

13. From Resistance to Renaissance 265

Conclusion 279

Acknowledgments 281

Appendix A: Essential AI Tools and Platforms 283

Appendix B: Master Implementation Framework 293

Notes 305

About the Author 317

Practical AI: A Playbook for Real Results

Let AI Be Your Coach isn't another theoretical exploration of artificial intelligence or a high-level overview of emerging technologies; instead, it's a comprehensive, practical playbook filled with proven prompts, strategies, and frameworks that will teach you how to communicate with AI effectively and transform it into your most valuable business partner.

I have been at the forefront of AI innovation and practical application for the last five years. In 2020, I built Rachel, the mortgage industry's first AI-powered digital human, pioneering the integration of conversational AI into financial services at a time when most businesses didn't even know about AI. Three years later, I developed InstaAI, a state-of-the-art generative AI platform that demonstrated how companies could harness the latest advances in artificial intelligence to drive real marketing improvements and transform sales productivity.

As an AI coach, I've had the privilege of speaking at national conferences, teaching thousands of professionals the concepts and practical applications of AI in everyday business operations, and advising numerous organizations on achieving significant efficiency gains through strategic AI implementation. These experiences have given me unique insights into not just what's technically possible with AI but, more importantly, how to bridge the gap between AI's potential and its practical, profitable application in real-world business scenarios.

The insights and strategies you'll find in these pages aren't based on speculation or abstract theory—they're tried-and-tested approaches that have been refined through countless implementations, workshops, and consulting engagements. Every prompt has been used successfully in real business situations. Every strategy has been validated through practical application. Every framework has helped actual entrepreneurs and professionals achieve measurable improvements in their operations and outcomes.

WHO THIS BOOK IS FOR

This book is designed for a diverse audience of professionals who recognize that AI represents a transformational opportunity but need practical guidance on how to harness it effectively. These professionals include

- **Entrepreneurs and business owners** who want to scale their operations without proportionally scaling their workload, who seek to make better strategic decisions faster, and who recognize that AI adoption isn't optional but need a systematic approach to implementation

- **Sales professionals** looking to supercharge their prospecting efforts, improve their conversion rates through AI-powered practice and coaching, and leverage data analytics to make smarter, more strategic sales decisions

- **Marketing professionals** who want to enhance their creative processes, optimize campaigns through intelligent testing and analysis, and deliver personalized experiences at scale without sacrificing authenticity or effectiveness

- **Business leaders and managers** seeking to build AI-powered knowledge bases that eliminate information silos, create more efficient decision-making processes, and develop their teams' capabilities more rapidly than traditional training methods allow

- **Consultants and service providers** who want to differentiate their offerings, deliver higher value to clients through AI-enhanced insights and solutions, and build more scalable service delivery models

The common thread among all these audiences is a recognition that AI isn't just another technology trend—it's a fundamental shift in how work gets done, decisions get made, and value gets created. However, recognizing this potential and knowing how to realize it are two very different challenges.

HOW THIS BOOK IS STRUCTURED

This book is organized around the key areas where AI coaching can create the most dramatic impact, building from foundational concepts to advanced applications.

Part 1 establishes the groundwork by showing how AI can transform organizations from the inside out. You'll learn to build AI-powered knowledge bases that turn organizational chaos into clarity, and you will discover how to position AI as your ultimate strategist, mentor, and coach for complex decision-making processes.

Part 2 focuses specifically on sales transformation, demonstrating how AI can serve as your ultimate rainmaker for prospecting and lead generation, function as an always-available practice partner for role-playing and skill development, and analyze data to inform more innovative sales strategies and decisions.

Part 3 explores marketing applications, showing how AI can serve as your creative collaborator for strategy and campaign development, optimize your marketing efforts through intelligent testing and learning, and enable personalization at a scale that was previously impossible without massive teams and budgets.

Part 4 addresses skill building and long-term success, demonstrating how AI can accelerate professional development and help you master complex skills faster than traditional approaches while also serving as an accountability partner and strategic advisor for goal achievement.

Part 5 looks toward the future, exploring the emerging world of agentic AI systems that can take independent action on your behalf and addressing the cultural and organizational shifts necessary to move from AI resistance to AI renaissance.

LEARNING THROUGH REAL-WORLD APPLICATION

Throughout this book, you'll encounter multiple real-world case studies that illustrate how theoretical concepts translate into practical applications. These aren't sanitized success stories but honest examinations of both victories and challenges, including the iterative process of learning to work effectively with AI.

We'll follow the transformative journeys of Sarah and Michael—two hypothetical entrepreneurs who begin their story as complete novices in the world of AI. Sarah, a real estate broker, and Michael, a mortgage lender, represent the thousands of professionals I've worked with who recognized AI's potential but needed practical guidance to harness it effectively. With curiosity, trial, and guidance, they navigate the learning curve, exploring the same tools, strategies, and prompts you'll discover in these pages.

As they apply what they learn, Sarah and Michael begin to unlock the true power of AI—not just as a set of tech tools but as a trusted partner in decision-making, creativity, and growth. Step-by-step, you'll see how they evolve—streamlining operations, improving customer experiences, and ultimately building smarter, stronger, and more scalable businesses. Their stories demonstrate that AI mastery isn't about technical expertise; it's about developing the right mindsets, approaches, and communication strategies.

Each chapter builds on the previous ones while remaining actionable on its own. You'll find specific prompts you can use immediately, detailed strategies you can implement step-by-step, and frameworks you can adapt to your unique situation and industry. The goal isn't just to inform you about what's possible—it's to give you the exact tools you need to make transformation happen in your own professional context.

The business world is changing faster than ever, and the entrepreneurs and professionals who thrive will be those who learn to harness AI not as a replacement for human intelligence and creativity but as an amplifier for both. The stories and strategies in this book are proof that this transformation is not only possible but practical, profitable, and personally fulfilling.

Your journey to letting AI be your coach starts now. Let's get to Chapter 1.

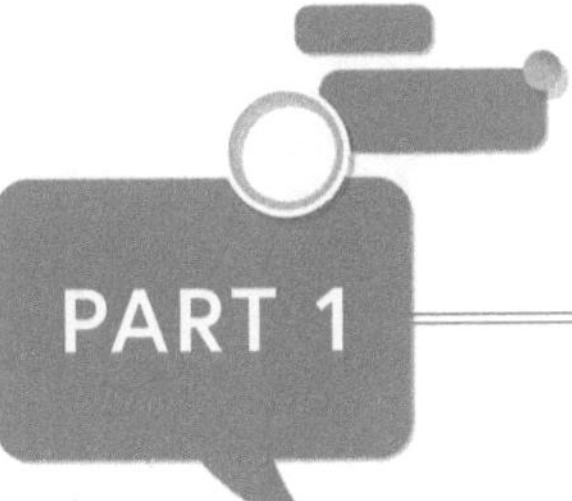

THE AI COACHING REVOLUTION

1

The AI Advantage: Transforming Organizations from the Inside Out

Sarah stared at her computer screen, surrounded by sticky notes that had somehow multiplied like rabbits across her desk. As a real estate broker managing fifteen agents, she'd mastered the art of juggling tasks—or so she thought. The morning's challenges included three new agent training sessions, a stack of contracts needing review, and what felt like a million unanswered client emails. Oh, and her coffee had gone cold. Again.

Three hundred miles away, Michael, a mortgage loan officer, was living a remarkably similar day, minus the cold coffee. He'd given up on coffee altogether and switched to energy drinks. Not the healthiest choice, but desperate times call for desperate measures.

Both Sarah and Michael had built successful businesses, but they'd hit the same wall that many growing companies face: There simply weren't enough hours in the day. You know that feeling when your to-do list starts looking more like a novel? They were living it.

Fast forward six months, and something remarkable had happened. Sarah's team was processing 40 percent more leads with better conversion rates. Michael was handling twice the loan applications while maintaining higher customer satisfaction scores. The game changer? They'd embraced AI as their digital coach and teammate. And no, it wasn't quite like having a robot assistant à la *iRobot*—though Sarah joked that her AI doesn't complain about her musical choices during late-night work sessions.

THE NEW REALITY OF BUSINESS

Remember when having a website was considered optional for small businesses? "My customers know where to find me" was a common refrain, usually uttered by the same folks who insisted social media was just a fad. That's where we are with AI today—it's transitioning from a nice-to-have to a must-have faster than you can say "digital transformation."

But here's the good news: You don't need a computer science degree or a Fortune 500 budget to leverage AI effectively. Gone are the days when implementing AI meant hiring a team of data scientists who speak in algorithms and dream in Python. Today's AI tools are more like having a really smart intern who works 24/7, doesn't need coffee breaks, and never complains about doing the same task a hundred times (though, unlike an intern, it won't laugh at your dad jokes—we're still working on that technology).

Let's take a moment to understand what this means for your business. Imagine having a team member who never sleeps (like that one overachiever we all know), learns from every interaction (faster than most of us learned to use the office coffee machine), provides consistent results (no

Monday morning blues here), and scales effortlessly (without requiring a bigger office or more snacks in the break room).

The magic happens when you combine those capabilities with human insight—which is exactly what Sarah and Michael discovered and what you'll learn throughout this book.

A QUICK PIT STOP: AI 101 (DON'T WORRY, I'LL KEEP IT BRIEF)

Before we dive deeper into transforming your organization, let's take a quick tour of the AI landscape. But this won't feel like that college computer science class you dozed through. Think of it as a quick guide to the tools you'll be using throughout this book.

FROM SCI-FI TO YOUR OFFICE: THE AI JOURNEY

Remember when AI was just something from movies, usually involving robots with an inexplicable desire to take over the world? Well, AI has come a long way since then, though it still hasn't developed any apocalyptic ambitions (as far as we know).

The real breakthrough came in 2022, with the public release of ChatGPT, which made everyone realize that AI wasn't just for tech giants anymore. Suddenly, the same technology that powers Tesla's self-driving cars and Netflix's eerily accurate recommendations was accessible to everyone—from Fortune 500 companies to small business owners who just want their email inboxes to be less overwhelming.

MEET YOUR NEW DIGITAL TEAMMATES: UNDERSTANDING LLMS

Some of the AI tools we'll be using throughout this book are called large language models (LLMs). Think of them as incredibly well-read assistants who have digested more information than any human could in a lifetime. The major players in this space include:

- **ChatGPT (by OpenAI):** The popular kid who made AI accessible to everyone. Available in free and premium versions (GPT-5).

- **Claude (by Anthropic):** Known for longer, more nuanced conversations and better at handling complex tasks. Think of it as ChatGPT's more analytical cousin.

- **Gemini (by Google):** The newest entrant, bringing Google's vast knowledge into the AI assistant space. Think of it as a new kid on the block.

These models can help with everything from writing emails to analyzing market trends—and even planning your kid's birthday party or that Paris trip you've been dreaming of.

A QUICK NOTE ON CAPABILITIES

While these AI tools are impressive, they do have their limitations. They can't always access real-time information. AI often has knowledge cutoff dates, which means their information may be outdated or incomplete for recent events. AI doesn't actually "understand" things the way humans do. Rather, AI processes patterns in text and generates responses based on statistical relationships learned during training. And don't forget the hallucinations. AI can be like that one colleague we all know who is confidently incorrect. That's why we need human oversight and guidance when using these AI tools.

Understanding these limitations is crucial because it helps us use AI tools more effectively. Think of them as extremely capable assistants rather than replacements for human judgment.

GENERATIVE AI: THE GAME CHANGER

You've probably heard the term "generative AI" thrown around in meetings or seen it in headlines. But what exactly is it? Think of it this way: If traditional AI is like a really smart calculator that can analyze existing information, generative AI (GenAI for short) is like having a creative partner who can produce new content from scratch. In fact, generative AI can write anything; from emails to marketing copy, it has you covered. GenAI can create images from text descriptions (think DALL·E, Midjourney) or generate code for software development. Some individuals have used GenAI to compose music and create videos from text prompts. Graphics and layouts can also be designed with the assistance of generative AI.

Let's look at some real-world examples of ways you might actually use AI:

- Content creation
  - Traditional AI: Can tell you if an email is likely to get a response
  - Generative AI: Can write the entire email for you, tailored to your recipient
- Analysis
  - Traditional AI: Can spot patterns in your sales data
  - Generative AI: Can analyze the data *and* write a detailed report with recommendations

- Customer service
    - ° Traditional AI: Can categorize customer inquiries
    - ° Generative AI: Can draft personalized responses and suggest solutions

Generative AI Is Revolutionary

What makes GenAI different is its ability to understand the context and create something new rather than just processing existing information. It's the difference between a tool that can spot spelling errors versus one that can rewrite your sentence to be more persuasive, a system that can label images versus one that can create brand-new images, or a program that can find information versus one that can explain complex topics in simple terms.

The tools we'll be using throughout this book—ChatGPT, Claude, and others—are all examples of GenAI. They're not just responding to your inputs; they're creating new, original outputs based on their training and your needs.

Now that we've covered the AI basics, including the game-changing capabilities of GenAI, let's get back to transforming your organization with these tools.

THE HIDDEN POWER OF AI IN DAILY OPERATIONS

What does AI really mean for your day-to-day operations? If you're imagining robots walking around your office delivering coffee and giving PowerPoint presentations, I hate to disappoint you—we're not quite there yet. But what we do have might be even better.

Consider this: Every day, your team makes hundreds of decisions, from how to respond to a client email to which leads to prioritize. Each decision draws upon their experience, knowledge, and sometimes (let's be honest) that extra shot of espresso. Now imagine augmenting that decision-making process with insights drawn from millions of similar situations. That's not science fiction—it's what AI does today.

Stitch Fix uses machine learning models and data science to interpret customer style surveys, purchase behavior, feedback, and body measurements to generate personalized clothing recommendations. Their AI and generative tools support stylists by narrowing down large assortments into curated selections for customers, enabling human stylists to add nuance, context, and a personal touch. More recently, they have also begun integrating AI into design and trend forecasting—helping to generate new styles and speed the response to market demand.[1]

This case study illustrates how AI can go beyond simple automation to create truly personalized experiences at scale, something that would be impossible with human effort alone. The real magic of AI isn't in replacing human intelligence; instead, the real magic is in amplifying it. Think of it as giving your team superpowers—minus the radioactive spider bites or expensive superhero suits.

ENHANCED DECISION-MAKING

We all know that gut feeling when making business decisions. Sometimes, it's spot on; other times, it's just that questionable hunch making its opinions known. AI brings data-driven insights to complement your intuition, like having a really smart friend who remembers everything they've ever read and can spot patterns in chaos.

Take pricing strategies for example. Instead of the traditional "competitor's price minus 10 percent" approach (we've all been there), AI can analyze market conditions, customer behavior, and historical data to suggest optimal pricing points. By utilizing AI for such a strategy, a retail chain might discover they are actually underpricing their premium products in certain markets—a realization that can lead to a revenue increase without losing customers.

PERSONALIZED LEARNING AND DEVELOPMENT

Remember the one-size-fits-all training programs of yesteryear? Those three-day workshops where the only thing people remembered was the free lunch? AI has transformed professional development into something actually, well, developmental.

Modern AI-powered learning platforms like CoachAI, a training platform created by me and the team at InstaAI, adapt to each individual's learning style, pace, and needs. They're like having a personal tutor who never runs out of patience and doesn't judge you for needing the same explanation three times.

When CoachAI was introduced to the loan officers at my company, InstaMortgage, they reported a significant improvement in their objection handling and closing techniques.

REAL-WORLD CASE STUDY
UPS' ORION System

UPS, the global shipping giant, provides an excellent example of how AI can optimize complex operations. In 2016, they fully deployed their On-Road Integrated Optimization and Navigation (ORION) system, an AI-powered route-optimization tool.

ORION uses advanced algorithms to calculate the most efficient delivery routes for UPS drivers, considering factors like traffic patterns, package priorities, and required delivery times. The system can evaluate 200,000 alternative route options for a single delivery route.

The results have been staggering. UPS estimates that ORION saves the company one hundred million miles driven annually, translating to a reduction of ten million gallons of fuel. This not only cuts costs but also significantly reduces the company's carbon footprint. In financial terms, UPS projects that ORION will save them $300–$400 million annually once it's fully implemented.

This case study demonstrates how AI can tackle complex logistical challenges, leading to significant improvements in efficiency, cost savings, and environmental impact.[2]

Let's move beyond the buzzwords and look at how AI actually changes the way people work.

COMING BACK TO SARAH AND MICHAEL

Sarah, our real estate broker from earlier, found that AI didn't just help with the obvious tasks like email responses and market analysis; it transformed how her entire team operated.

Her newest agent, Tom, used AI tools to practice difficult client conversations before having them in real life. "It's like having a flight simulator for real estate," he explained. "You can crash and burn without actually losing a client." The result? Tom reached his first-year targets in just seven months, and more importantly, he didn't develop an ulcer in the process.

Meanwhile, Michael, our loan officer friend, discovered that AI could help humanize his work, not just automate it. By handling the number crunching and document processing, AI freed up his time, which allowed him to spend more time understanding his clients' stories and dreams. "I'm having deeper conversations about people's life goals," he said, "instead of just talking about interest rates and credit scores."

THE IMPLEMENTATION REALITY CHECK

I know what you're thinking: Implementing AI sounds great, but isn't it complicated? Won't it require a PhD in computer science and a budget that makes your accountant cry?

The short answer is no. The longer answer is definitely no, because modern AI tools are designed to be user-friendly. If you can use a smartphone or navigate the recommendations on Netflix, you can use AI in your business.

Start small. Pick one process that's currently eating up too much of your time. Maybe it's sorting through emails, qualifying leads, or preparing initial client presentations. Find an AI tool that addresses that specific need. It's like learning to swim: You start in the shallow end, not attempting to cross the English Channel.

A boutique marketing agency began its AI journey with a simple goal: speed up its content creation process. They started using AI to generate first drafts of social media posts. Within weeks, they were producing three times the content in half the time.[3]

MAKING AI WORK IN YOUR ORGANIZATION

But what happens after you decide to bring AI into your business? It's a bit like bringing home a new pet: exciting and full of potential, but you need to know how to train it and integrate it into your household. Unlike a pet, though, AI won't chew your shoes or wake you up at 3 a.m. for attention.

THE INTEGRATION DANCE

The key to successful AI implementation lies in the Integration Dance—a carefully choreographed process that involves three main steps: preparation, introduction, and adaptation. Think of it as a waltz, not a chaotic Bollywood dance at a wedding reception.

First comes preparation. This means taking a good, hard look at your current processes. I once worked with a sales team that wanted to implement AI for lead scoring. When we started mapping their current process, we discovered they had seven different ways of categorizing leads—none of which were documented. As their sales director put it, "We weren't organizing leads; we were creating elaborate chaos."

The introduction phase is where many organizations stumble, usually because they try to do too much too fast. Rather than attempting to revolutionize their entire sales process overnight, this same sales team wisely chose to start small. We implemented the AI lead scoring system for just their inbound marketing leads—roughly 30 percent of their total volume. This allowed the team to learn how the AI worked, understand its recommendations, and build confidence with the technology without overwhelming their established workflows or disrupting relationships with existing prospects.

Adaptation is the ongoing process of adjusting and optimizing your AI implementation. This is where the magic really happens. After three months, the sales team discovered something unexpected: The AI was exceptionally accurate at identifying leads who were likely to purchase within thirty days, but it initially struggled with long-term prospects who required six-to-twelve-month nurturing cycles. They adapted by creating two distinct scoring tracks: "hot leads" for immediate follow-up and "warm cultivation" for longer-term relationship building. This adaptation led to a 28 percent increase in conversion rates and, more importantly, helped sales reps focus their time more effectively on the right prospects at the right time.

THE HUMAN SIDE OF AI INTEGRATION

Here's a truth that often gets lost in the excitement about AI: The technology is only as effective as the humans using it. This brings us to what I call the three Cs of human–AI integration: confidence building, clear communication, and continuous learning.

Start by letting your team experiment with AI in low-stakes situations for confidence building. Sarah had her agents use AI to draft property descriptions for imaginary houses before moving on to actual listings. This not only built confidence but led to some hilariously creative descriptions. "I never knew I needed to list a house with a 'quantum meditation garden' until the AI suggested it," one agent said.

Clear communication proved crucial when Michael introduced AI tools to his loan processing team. He established a shared understanding of how to effectively prompt and interact with their AI assistants. "We learned that asking AI to 'make this better' was about as helpful as telling a chef to 'make it tasty,'" he explained. "But when we clearly communicated our needs, like 'simplify this mortgage term for a first-time homebuyer,' the results were remarkable." (Read more about this in the prompt-engineering section later in the chapter.)

Continuous learning emerged as the cornerstone of successful integration. A regional insurance agency embraced this principle by creating weekly AI discovery sessions where team members shared their best findings and funniest AI interactions. "We turned learning into an adventure," their training director shared. "One week, someone discovered that AI could explain complex policies using superhero analogies. Now, 'The Incredible Insurance Hulk' is part of our regular training vocabulary!"

MEASURING SUCCESS: BEYOND THE NUMBERS

When it comes to measuring the success of your AI implementation, the obvious metrics are important: efficiency gains, cost savings, and revenue increases.

REAL-WORLD CASE STUDY
Coca-Cola's AI-Powered Vending Machines

Consider the case of Coca-Cola, a company that's been around for over a century but is still finding innovative ways to use AI. In 2018, they introduced AI-powered vending machines in Australia and New Zealand. These smart machines can change their digital displays based on the weather, time of day, or even nearby events. On a hot day, they might promote cold drinks more prominently. During a local sporting event, they could display team colors and relevant promotions.

The results were impressive. Coca-Cola reported a 15 percent increase in revenue from these AI-powered machines compared to traditional vending machines. But it wasn't just about making more profit from selling more drinks. The AI also helped reduce maintenance costs by predicting when machines needed restocking or repairs. For example, they saw an 18 percent reduction in restocking visits, which led to a decrease in operational expenses.[4]

But some of the most valuable impacts aren't as easily quantifiable. A small law firm hired me to implement AI for contract review, expecting to see time savings. They got that—contract review time decreased by 22 percent. But the unexpected benefit came in the form of job satisfaction. Junior lawyers, previously drowning in mundane contract reviews, now had time to work on more challenging aspects of cases. As one partner noted, "We didn't just get faster; we got happier."

PLANNING YOUR AI JOURNEY: THE ROAD AHEAD

AI isn't like flipping a switch—it's more like planning a road trip. You need a destination in mind, but you also need to be prepared for interesting detours along the way.

Start by asking yourself these three questions:

1. What processes in your business feel like running on a treadmill—lots of effort but not enough forward movement?

2. Where do you or your team spend time on tasks that don't directly contribute to growth or customer satisfaction?

3. What information or insights do you wish you had but can't gather with your current resources?

The answers to these questions become what I call your transformation triggers—the points where AI can create the most immediate and meaningful impact.

YOUR FIRST STEPS: A THIRTY-DAY LAUNCH PLAN

Think of the first thirty days of AI implementation as your intelligence incubation period. During this time, you're not just implementing technology; you're cultivating a new way of thinking about your business. This isn't a rigid schedule; rather, it's a flexible framework you can adapt to your specific needs.

Week one is the discovery phase. During this week, spend time observing and documenting. Pay attention to where time gets spent, where bottlenecks occur, and where your team expresses the most frustration. One CEO I worked with kept what she called her "friction journal," noting every time she or her team hit a procedural speed bump.

Weeks two and three focus on selective implementation. Like Sarah and Michael did, start with one clearly defined area. Maybe it's email management, lead qualification, or customer support. The key is to choose something specific enough to measure but significant enough to matter.

The final week is your evaluation and expansion phase. By now, you should have some initial results and insights. Use this time to assess what's working, what needs adjustment, and where you might want to expand next.

THE PATH FORWARD

Remember, implementing AI in your organization isn't about replacing human intelligence; it's about augmenting it. Think of AI as giving your team superpowers, allowing them to work smarter, not harder.

Your journey with AI will be unique to your organization. Some days, it will feel like you're living in the future; other days, you might wonder if your AI assistant needs a coffee break. That's normal. The key is to maintain your sense of humor, stay focused on your goals, and remember that every successful business transformation started with a single step.

Remember, you aren't just adding technology to your business; you are transforming how you think about what's possible. The real power isn't in the AI itself; it's in how it lets us be more capable humans.

Understanding Prompt Engineering: The Key to Unlocking Generative AI's Potential

Prompt engineering is the practice of crafting effective instructions (or "prompts") to guide GenAI models—like ChatGPT, Claude, or Gemini—to produce accurate, relevant, and useful responses. Think of it as giving precise directions to a GPS—the clearer and more specific your input, the better the AI's output. For example, asking a model, "Tell me about space" will yield a broad, general answer, while refining the prompt to "Explain the history of space exploration from the 1960s to today, including key missions and discoveries" ensures a more targeted response.

Prompt engineering is essential for optimizing AI tools across industries, from writing and research to coding, marketing, and business automation. Without well-structured prompts, AI can generate vague, irrelevant, or even incorrect information, a phenomenon known as "hallucination."

To master prompt engineering, follow these best practices: Be specific, provide context, use step-by-step instructions, define the format of the response, and iterate for refinement. A useful framework for structuring prompts is the CRISPE method:

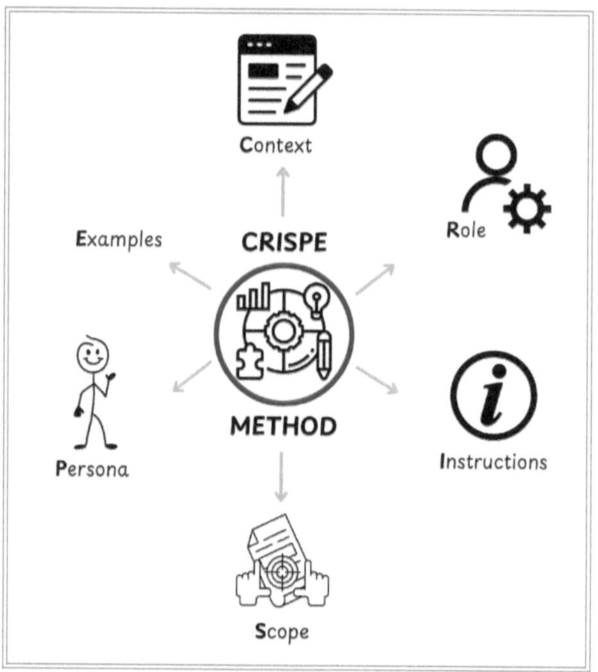

- **Context**—Set the background (e.g., "You are an expert in digital marketing").

- **Role**—Assign a persona to the AI (e.g., "Act as a mortgage loan officer").

- **Instructions**—Clearly outline the task (e.g., "Explain the impact of interest rates on homebuyers in 2025").

- **Scope**—Define length, format, or depth (e.g., "Provide a concise, 300-word response with bullet points").

- **Persona**—Specify the tone, style, or expertise level for the response (e.g., "Speak like a high-energy personal trainer who's always motivating their clients").

- **Examples**—Offer samples to guide AI (e.g., "Similar to the style of a *Forbes* article").

Let's apply the CRISPE method to creating an ad for a backpack for a Gen Z audience.

1. BASIC PROMPT

Most people start here:

Prompt:

Write Facebook ad copy for colorful backpacks targeting Gen Z.

Looks simple, right? But this kind of prompt often leads to forgettable, generic content.

ChatGPT Response:

Headline:

Make School Cool Again!

Text:

Hey Gen Z! Ready to upgrade your style? Our colorful backpacks bring flair, function, and fun. Whether you're heading to class or hitting the streets, do it with confidence.

Water-resistant, lightweight, and built for your vibe.

Call to Action (CTA):

Shop Now

Why It Falls Flat:

- Too vague

- No product details

- No tone guidance

- Feels generic, not Gen Z–specific

2. ADD SPECIFIC DETAILS

Now, let's add some context so ChatGPT understands what makes the product special.

Improved Prompt:

Write Facebook ad copy for colorful backpacks targeting Gen Z.

The backpacks feature bold color-block designs and are made from recycled materials. They're lightweight, water-resistant, and priced at $39.99.

The brand voice is bold, expressive, and eco-conscious. The main selling point is vibrant self-expression with sustainable function.

ChatGPT Response:

Primary Text:

Make a bold move.

Our color-block backpacks are loud, light, and made for *your* vibe. Crafted with recycled materials and priced under $40, they're the perfect mix of fashion and function.

Headline:

Express Yourself. Sustainably.

CTA:

Get Yours Now

What's Better:

- Includes product details and pricing

- Reflects some brand values

- Starts to tap into Gen Z tone

What's Still Missing:

- No structure or step-by-step guidance

- No control over tone or flow

- No examples to anchor the style

3. ADD STEP-BY-STEP INSTRUCTIONS

Next, we guide ChatGPT on *how* to write the ad copy.

Prompt (with Steps):

Write Facebook ad copy for colorful backpacks targeting Gen Z.

The backpacks feature bold color-block designs and are made from recycled materials. They're lightweight, water-resistant, and priced at $39.99.

The brand voice is bold, expressive, and eco-conscious. The main selling point is vibrant self-expression with sustainable function.

Steps:

1. Start with an attention-grabbing headline that emphasizes individuality.
2. Write a compelling first line that taps into Gen Z's desire for self-expression.
3. Present the key features and benefits, emphasizing sustainability.
4. Include a clear call to action.
5. Keep the tone playful, confident, and relatable.
6. Use emoji strategically to match Gen Z energy.

ChatGPT Response:

Primary Text:

Stand out without saying a word.

Our vibrant backpacks are built for self-expression and made from recycled materials—because saving the planet *is* cool. Lightweight, water-resistant, and just $39.99.

Headline:

Your Bag, Your Energy

CTA:

Grab Yours Today

What's Better:

- Structure is cleaner
- Product features are emphasized
- Tone is improving

What Could Be Stronger:

- Still a bit flat on voice

- Emoji feel minimal

- Doesn't quite capture Gen Z quirk or energy

4. ADD EXAMPLES TO ANCHOR THE TONE

Now, we add an example to show exactly what kind of output we want.

Prompt (with Steps + Example):

> Write Facebook ad copy for colorful backpacks targeting Gen Z.
>
> The backpacks feature bold color-block designs and are made from recycled materials. They're lightweight, water-resistant, and priced at $39.99.
>
> The brand voice is bold, expressive, and eco-conscious. The main selling point is vibrant self-expression with sustainable function.
>
> **Steps:**
> 1. Start with an attention-grabbing headline that emphasizes individuality.
> 2. Write a compelling first line that taps into Gen Z's desire for self-expression.
> 3. Present the key features and benefits, emphasizing sustainability.
> 4. Include a clear call to action.
> 5. Keep the tone playful, confident, and relatable.
> 6. Use emoji strategically to match Gen Z energy.
>
> **Example:**
>
> Not Just a Backpack. A Whole Mood.

> Say goodbye to boring bags. Our color-block backpacks are bright, bold, and built from recycled materials.
>
> Lightweight, water-resistant, and unapologetically you.

ChatGPT Response:

Primary Text:

Why blend in when you can stand *way* out?

These bold, color-block backpacks are your new favorite statement piece. Recycled materials? Check. Water-resistant? Of course. Lightweight for your daily hustle? Always.

All for $39.99—because style shouldn't cost the planet.

Headline:

Pack Loud. Live Proud.

CTA:

Shop the Vibe

Why This Is Strong:

- Tone matches Gen Z energy
- Product benefits + brand values are clear
- Strategic emoji use
- Fun, expressive, and on-brand

5. FINAL PROMPT (WITH FULL FORMAT AND FINAL OUTPUT)

Here's the polished, ready-to-use version of the perfect prompt.

Final Prompt:

Write Facebook ad copy for colorful backpacks targeting Gen Z.

The backpacks feature bold color-block designs and are made from recycled materials. They're lightweight, water-resistant, and priced at $39.99.

The brand voice is bold, expressive, and eco-conscious. The main selling point is vibrant self-expression with sustainable function.

Steps:
1. Start with an attention-grabbing headline that emphasizes individuality.
2. Write a compelling first line that taps into Gen Z's desire for self-expression.
3. Present the key features and benefits, emphasizing sustainability.
4. Include a clear call to action.
5. Keep the tone playful, confident, and relatable.
6. Use emoji strategically to match Gen Z energy.

Example:

Not Just a Backpack. A Whole Mood.

Say goodbye to boring bags. Our color-block backpacks are bright, bold, and built from recycled materials.

Lightweight, water-resistant, and unapologetically you.

Response Format:
- **Primary Text:** [Main ad copy with emoji]
- **Headline:** [Attention-grabbing headline]
- **Description:** [2–3 lines of supporting text]
- **Call to Action:** [Button text]

ChatGPT Response (Final):

Primary Text:

This isn't just a backpack—it's your vibe in bag form.

Rock bold color blocks, stay light on your feet, and rep eco-conscious choices every day. Made from recycled materials, water-resistant, and under $40.

Who says functional can't be fabulous?

Headline:

Backpacks That Speak You

Description

Sustainably made, colorfully loud, and totally you.

Perfect for campus, travel, and turning heads.

Call to Action:

Grab Yours Now

FINAL TAKEAWAY

If you want high-quality, viral content from ChatGPT, you need to lead with clarity. AI brings creativity—but only if you bring *direction*.

Use this structure every time:

- Be specific.

- Break it down.

- Give examples.

- Set expectations.

This way, you're not just asking for "ad copy"; you're building a blueprint that turns AI into your sharpest creative partner.

2

From Chaos to Clarity: Building an AI-Powered Knowledge Base

Picture this: It's 9:47 p.m., and somewhere in Silicon Valley, a software engineer is hunting through Slack channels, trying to find that one crucial piece of code someone shared "a few months ago." Meanwhile, in Chicago, a solo financial advisor is diving into her fifteenth browser tab, searching for that perfect market analysis she knows she saved "somewhere." And in a Houston office building, a project manager is quietly wondering if it would be professionally acceptable to scream, "WHERE IS THAT DOCUMENT?" at full volume.

Sound familiar? Welcome to the modern workplace, where finding information often feels like trying to find your keys while running late—you know they exist, you just can't remember where you put them.

THE HIDDEN COST OF INFORMATION HIDE-AND-SEEK

Let's talk about the elephant in the room—or more accurately, the elephantine cost of scattered information. According to a McKinsey report, employees spend an average of 1.8 hours every day searching and gathering information.[1] That's nine hours a week—enough time to watch the entire *Lord of the Rings* trilogy.

But the real cost goes beyond time. When a sales rep can't quickly find the latest pricing information, when a customer service agent has to put a client on hold to dig through email threads, or when a marketing team recreates content because they can't find the original, these aren't just inconveniences; they're death by a thousand paper cuts to your organization's productivity.

Consider this hypothetical scenario: A midsize software company discovers their support team is maintaining three different versions of their troubleshooting guide: one in Google Docs, one in Notion, and one that mysteriously existed only on someone named Dave's laptop. The kicker? No one named Dave has worked at the company for the past two years.

REAL-WORLD CASE STUDY
IBM Watson Assistant at Crédit Mutuel

Crédit Mutuel, one of France's largest banks, partnered with IBM to deploy Watson Assistant to support its twenty thousand customer advisors. The AI system was trained on thousands of documents and client interactions to help employees quickly access information, answer customer questions, and reduce repetitive tasks.

These were the results reported by IBM:

- Customer advisors handled inquiries 60 percent faster by using Watson to retrieve relevant information.

- Over 150,000 conversations per month were supported by Watson Assistant.
- The tool improved employee productivity while allowing advisors to focus on higher-value, personalized client interactions.

This case demonstrates how AI-powered knowledge systems can reduce time spent searching for information and improve both employee effectiveness and client satisfaction—very similar to the goals Watson Workspace once aimed to achieve.[2]

THE THREE PILLARS OF KNOWLEDGE MANAGEMENT

Think of your organizational knowledge like preparing a gourmet meal: You need a base to build from—a kitchen with all the necessary appliances and tools, high-quality ingredients, and a chef who can turn those ingredients into something delicious. For your organization's knowledge base, you need the three A's in order to create your master knowledge base:

1. **Accessibility:** It's not enough for information to exist—it needs to be findable. Imagine a car manufacturer's engineering team learning the hard way when they realize different departments had solved the same problem three times because no one could find the original solution. The solution? An AI-powered knowledge base that would be "Google for their company."

2. **Accuracy:** Having information is one thing; having the right information is another. A financial services firm might discover they had five different versions of their client onboarding process, ranging from "slightly outdated" to "this might as well be written in hieroglyphics."

3. **Actionability:** Information should lead to action, not just exist in digital limbo. When HubSpot revamped its knowledge-management system, it focused on making information actionable. The result? Their new employees were reaching productivity milestones 34 percent faster than before the implementation.[3]

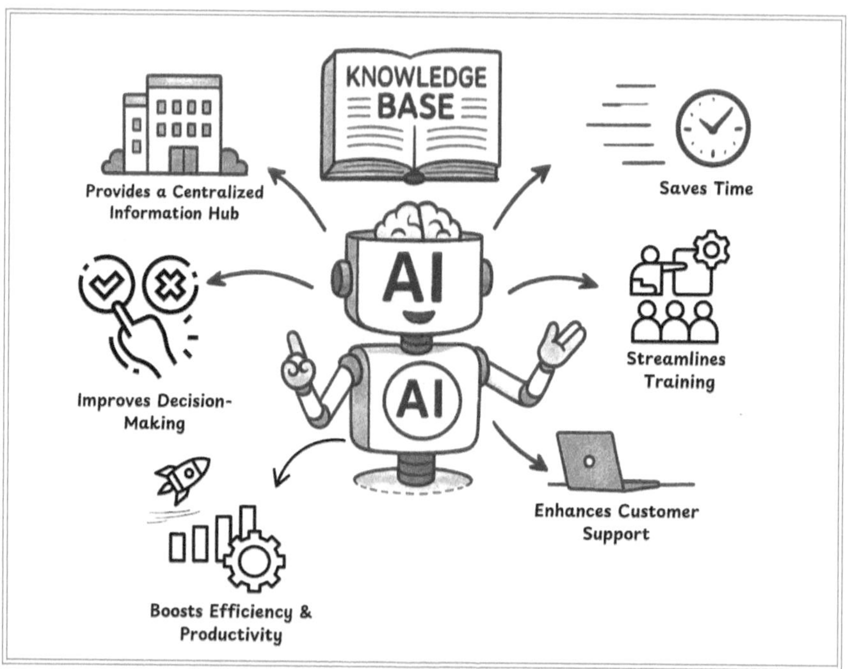

BUILDING YOUR KNOWLEDGE FOUNDATION: WHERE TO BEGIN

Remember the last time you tried to organize your closet? You likely started with good intentions, pulled everything out, and somewhere around hour three, you were sitting in a pile of clothes, wondering why you own seven different black turtlenecks when your name is not Steve Jobs. Building a knowledge base can feel similarly overwhelming at first. But unlike that pile of questionable fashion choices, this is one organizational challenge that pays dividends.

The Great Knowledge Audit: What Do You Actually Have?

First things first—you need to know what you're working with. Think of this as taking inventory, except instead of counting physical items, you're cataloging your organization's collective brain. Here's where it gets interesting (and sometimes scary).

A software start-up I worked with recently began its knowledge audit with supreme confidence. "We're pretty organized," their CTO assured me. Three days later, he called back sounding slightly shell-shocked. They'd discovered the following in their audit:

- Seven different versions of their coding standards document

- A crucial API (application programming interface) documentation that only existed in one developer's personal notes

- An entire Git repository that everyone had forgotten about

- A Slack channel dedicated to sharing important information that no one had posted in since 2021

- Mysteriously, a very detailed guide to making the perfect cup of coffee that no one admitted to writing

The point isn't to shame anyone (we've all been there) but to recognize that information has a way of multiplying and also hiding in plain sight. As one project manager put it, "Documents are like rabbits: Leave them unmanaged for a while, and suddenly you have way more than you started with."

REAL-WORLD CASE STUDY
Airbnb's Knowledge Repository

At Airbnb, the Data team faced a growing challenge: how to ensure that valuable insights uncovered by one team member could be efficiently shared and leveraged across the organization. In the early days, when the team was small, informal sharing methods—such as emails, presentations, and Google Docs—were sufficient. However, as the company expanded, this ad hoc approach led to inefficiencies.

A case in point was the work of a new data scientist who wanted to build upon a colleague's research on host rejections. She struggled to find relevant work, sifted through scattered files, and ultimately had to spend time reproducing the original analysis before she could even begin her own. This fragmented process slowed down decision-making and led to repeated work rather than cumulative knowledge-building.

Recognizing the inefficiencies, the Data team sought a more structured way to manage and share research findings. They identified five guiding principles: Research should be (1) reproducible, ensuring no outdated or forked versions; (2) high in quality, with a review process to check accuracy; (3) consumable, meaning insights should be easy to understand and visually consistent; (4) discoverable, allowing anyone in the company to find relevant work; and (5) educational, helping team members build on each other's techniques. With these principles in mind, they examined existing tools that addressed some of these issues but found that no single solution fully met their needs.

The team's answer was to create an internal system, which they named the Knowledge Repo. This platform streamlined the process of contributing, reviewing, and distributing research in a standardized format. By integrating elements from existing tools—such as structured documentation, code repositories, and intuitive navigation—the Knowledge Repo enabled Airbnb's data scientists to collaborate more effectively.

Now, instead of struggling to locate previous analyses or recreate work from scratch, team members can quickly find, update, and build upon prior research, significantly improving efficiency and the speed of decision-making across the company.[4]

THE KNOWLEDGE NETWORK EFFECT

Think of your knowledge audit as a digital archaeological dig: You're not just looking for documents; you're uncovering the artifacts of your organization's thinking and decision-making processes.

One company I worked with found email templates buried in a personal folder of an employee who had left the company two years prior. A real estate agent found a presentation format in a folder on the company's server title "Random Stuff." And one lending officer I worked with found a spreadsheet in their shared drive that perfectly documented seasonal lending patterns, a spreadsheet that they'd been recreating every quarter instead of just updating the original.

But the real revelation came when these companies started understanding what I call the Knowledge Network Effect: how different pieces of information connect and enhance each other. A client meeting note might contain the key to understanding a successful sales strategy. A casual email exchange might reveal the perfect way to handle a common customer objection.

The Knowledge Network Effect thrives on the principle that information gains exponential value when it is connected rather than existing in isolation. This effect is especially powerful in fast-moving industries like real estate, finance, and technology, where decision-making depends on synthesizing multiple data points. For instance, a real estate agency tracking client preferences might notice, through a combination of call transcripts and property tour feedback, that buyers in a certain income bracket are drawn to homes with flexible workspaces. Alone, a single note from an agent might not reveal much, but when layered with market trends and sales outcomes, a clearer picture emerges—allowing the firm to refine its marketing, pricing strategies, and inventory selection.

Companies that actively harness the Knowledge Network Effect often see significant improvements in efficiency, innovation, and competitive advantage. Google's internal "g2g" (Googler-to-Googler) system is a real-world example where employees document solutions to problems in a shared knowledge repository. Instead of reinventing the wheel, employees can build upon past experiences, reducing time spent troubleshooting and enhancing collaboration. When businesses prioritize connecting information across teams, they don't just store knowledge—they amplify its impact, turning it into a strategic advantage.

THE TOOL SELECTION CHRONICLES: FINDING YOUR PERFECT MATCH

After implementing AI for basic tasks, Sarah faced a new challenge: Her team's improved efficiency was generating more information than ever. Meanwhile, Michael was discovering that his AI-enhanced workflow was creating valuable insights he needed to capture and share.

Their experiences highlight a crucial truth: As your business becomes more AI-enabled, your need for effective knowledge management grows exponentially. Let's see how they, and others, navigated the tool selection process.

The Tool Spectrum: From Simple to Sophisticated

Sarah's journey started with a simple question: Where did they put that really successful property listing template that AI helped them create? After the third time recreating the same template, she knew she needed a system. But with options ranging from simple note-taking apps to enterprise-level knowledge-management systems, she didn't know where to begin.

"I felt like I was speed dating software." She laughed. "Some were trying too hard to impress me with features I'd never use, others were clearly not ready for a serious relationship, and a few were just . . . well, let's say they had a great personality."

The Starting Point Solutions

Think of these as your starter home in the knowledge-management world. Tools like Notion, Evernote, or Google Drive with organized folder structures serve as entry-level solutions. They're not fancy, but they get the job done for small teams beginning their knowledge-management journey.

These tools work well for capturing and organizing AI-generated content, templates, and insights. For example, a small marketing agency might use Notion to store AI-created social media templates, campaign strategies, and client communication frameworks. Team members can easily search for and reuse successful AI-assisted campaigns, turning one-time AI outputs into reusable organizational knowledge. The simplicity allows teams to start building knowledge-management habits without overwhelming complexity.

The Midrange Marvels

These solutions—tools like Confluence, GitBook, or well-configured SharePoint systems—offer more sophisticated features for growing organizations. They're like moving into a nice condo: more features and better organization but without overwhelming complexity.

These platforms excel at creating structured knowledge bases with advanced search capabilities, user permissions, and integration options. A consulting firm might use Confluence to build a comprehensive knowledge repository where AI-generated research summaries, client solutions, and best practices are categorized by industry and service type. Team members can quickly locate relevant past work, and the AI-enhanced search functionality helps surface related content that might not be immediately obvious. The system becomes particularly powerful when integrated with other business tools, automatically capturing and organizing insights from various AI-powered workflows.

The Enterprise Powerhouses

At the sophisticated end of the spectrum sit comprehensive platforms like Microsoft Viva, Guru, or custom-built knowledge-management systems. These solutions offer advanced AI integration, automated content curation, real-time collaboration features, and extensive analytics capabilities.

These systems can automatically capture knowledge from multiple sources, use AI to suggest relevant content during workflows, and provide detailed insights into how organizational knowledge is being used and evolving. For instance, a large financial services firm might implement a system that automatically captures insights from AI-assisted client interactions, categorizes them by service type and client profile, and surfaces relevant information to advisors in real time during client meetings. The system learns from successful interactions and continuously improves its recommendations, creating a self-improving knowledge ecosystem that amplifies both AI capabilities and human expertise across the organization.

REAL-WORLD CASE STUDY
Spotify's Backstage

Spotify, the music streaming giant, faced growing complexity in managing its microservices architecture and the knowledge around it. To address this, they developed Backstage, an open-source developer portal that centralizes technical documentation, APIs, deployment pipelines, and monitoring tools into a single, unified platform. Its "golden path" approach provides standardized guidance for developers, reducing friction in onboarding and daily workflows.

The results have been tangible. At Spotify, new engineers now reach their tenth pull request in under twenty days, compared to about sixty days before Backstage. Frequent Backstage users also produce over twice as many code changes, deploy software twice as often, and achieve 17 percent faster cycle times, with those deployments staying in production three times longer.

This case illustrates how a well-designed internal knowledge- and service-management system can significantly improve developer productivity, reduce onboarding hurdles, and enhance reliability in tech-heavy environments.[5]

THE INTEGRATION DANCE: MAKING YOUR TOOLS WORK TOGETHER

Remember that AI assistant Sarah implemented in Chapter 1? Now it needed to play nicely with her new knowledge-management system. The integration process reminded her of hosting a dinner party where not all the guests know each other—some hit it off immediately, while others need a bit more introduction.

Michael faced a similar challenge. His AI tools were generating valuable insights about loan processing patterns, but he needed a way to capture and organize this information automatically. "It was like having a brilliant assistant who spoke a different language," he explained. "I needed to find a way to translate and preserve their insights."

Here's where the magic of modern integration capabilities comes into play. Using tools like Zapier or native integrations, both Sarah and Michael created workflows that automatically captured AI-generated insights, categorized information based on content, tagged documents for easy retrieval, and notified relevant team members about new information.

One particularly clever solution came from Sarah's team. Any time the AI identified a particularly successful client interaction or sales approach, the team created a new knowledge base entry and notified all agents.

THE HUMAN SIDE OF KNOWLEDGE MANAGEMENT: MAKING IT STICK

Three months into her knowledge base implementation, Sarah faced an unexpected challenge. While her AI systems were dutifully capturing and organizing information, she noticed some veteran agents were still hoarding their best practices in personal notebooks and private folders. "It was like having a potluck dinner where some people refused to share their recipes," she said with a sigh.

Michael, meanwhile, had the opposite problem. His enthusiasm for documenting everything led to what he now laughingly calls "The Great Knowledge Flood of 2024." "I was so excited about capturing everything that I created a digital version of my grandmother's attic—full of potentially valuable stuff, but good luck finding anything specific."

Their experiences highlight a crucial truth: The world's most sophisticated knowledge-management system won't help if people either won't use it or don't use it effectively. Let's explore how they and others transformed their knowledge bases from digital filing cabinets into living, breathing assets.

THE PSYCHOLOGY OF SHARING

Research in organizational psychology has revealed that reluctance to share knowledge often stems from a phenomenon known as "expertise insurance"—the idea that holding onto unique knowledge makes someone indispensable. A common realization within tech environments is that while one might initially think being the sole expert on critical, legacy systems secures job value, in reality, being known as the person who empowers others by sharing that knowledge makes one far more valuable.[6]

Knowledge hoarding inevitably impacts customers, leading to a poorer perception and experience with the organization. Conversely, fostering knowledge-sharing enhances team collaboration, which, as reported by the Institute for Collaborative Working, boosts customer satisfaction by 41 percent.[7]

Sarah tackled this challenge with the "Knowledge Karma" system. Any time someone's shared knowledge led to a successful sale, both the contributor and the user got public recognition and a small bonus. "Suddenly, my veterans weren't just sharing their knowledge; they were competing to see whose insights were most valuable," she said with a grin.

THE ART OF USEFUL DOCUMENTATION

Michael's journey from knowledge hoarder to knowledge curator came with important lessons. "I had to learn the difference between capturing information and creating useful knowledge," he explained. His breakthrough came when he established a simple three-question test for any new addition to his knowledge base:

1. Will this help someone make a better decision?

2. Could I understand this at 4:30 on a Friday afternoon?

3. Would this have saved me time when I was starting out?

If the answer to at least two of these questions wasn't yes, the information either needed reformatting or didn't belong in the knowledge base.

A simple but effective tagging system looks like this:

- Must know: Essential information for daily operations

- Good to know: Helpful context and background

- Nice to know: Interesting but not critical information

It's like Netflix categories for business knowledge: You can binge on the deep cuts if you want, but the hit shows are easy to find.

MAKING KNOWLEDGE FLOW: THE RIVER, NOT THE LAKE

Sarah's most recent innovation came from an unexpected source: her teenage son's Spotify playlist. "He never has to search for new music; it just flows to him based on what he likes," she observed. This inspired her to work with her AI tools to create "knowledge streams"—customized feeds of relevant information pushed to each agent based on their current deals, client types, and past interests.

Michael adapted this concept for his loan business, creating automated digests of relevant market trends, regulation updates, and successful case studies. "It's like having a really smart news editor who knows exactly what you need to see," he explained. His favorite feature? The AI-powered "You Might Have Missed This" feature that flags relevant information from the knowledge base.

THE EVOLUTION IMPERATIVE: YOUR KNOWLEDGE BASE OF TOMORROW

As we look ahead, I believe we're entering what I have termed the Coaching Convergence Era—where AI and human coaching abilities create the

Synergy Effect. This powerful combination leverages AI's vast data processing and pattern recognition capabilities with human coaches' emotional intelligence, contextual understanding, and intuitive wisdom to create outcomes neither could achieve alone. This isn't just about organizing information—it's about fundamentally transforming how organizations develop and share knowledge.

Research from the National Academies of Sciences, Engineering, and Medicine emphasizes the importance of continuous learning and adaptation in the workforce.[8] As AI systems evolve, so, too, must employees' skills and knowledge. Implementing robust training programs and fostering a lifelong learning culture is essential to ensure that workers can effectively collaborate with AI technologies and thrive in an AI-enhanced work environment.

THE INTEGRATION INTELLIGENCE PROTOCOL

Successfully implementing a modern knowledge base requires a systematic approach to blending AI capabilities with human expertise.

My three-step framework for this integration focuses on mapping existing knowledge flows, identifying AI augmentation opportunities, and establishing feedback loops for continuous improvement. This creates the Harmony Effect, where each element enhances the other.

Research from *Nature Human Behaviour* provides nuanced insights into human–AI collaboration. The study found that while human–AI teams often underperform compared to AI alone in decision-making tasks, they show significant promise in creative endeavors.[9] This suggests that the effectiveness of integrating AI with human knowledge systems varies depending on the nature of the task.

YOUR IMPLEMENTATION ROAD MAP

Let's conclude with a systematic three-step approach to implementing your modern knowledge base:

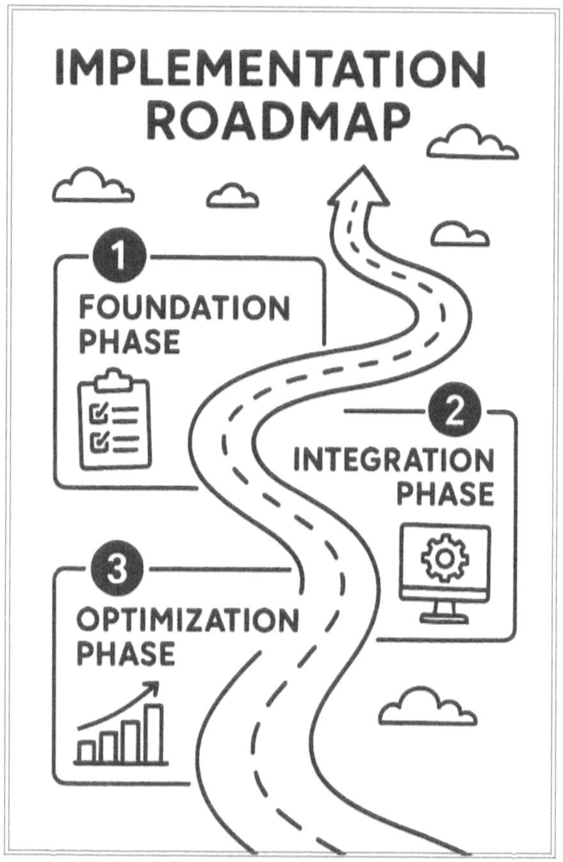

1. **The foundation phase:** Before you start feeding data into your AI system, you need to *know what you know.* That starts with a good old-fashioned audit—but don't worry, this one's more Indiana Jones than IRS. Begin by mapping your current knowledge landscape: what documents exist, where they live, who created them, and whether anyone actually uses them. Talk to your people—yes,

real humans! Interview stakeholders across departments to uncover tribal knowledge that's never been written down but is crucial to day-to-day operations. Your goal here is to surface the content that's most frequently used, frequently requested, or frequently misunderstood. Whether it's onboarding procedures, product specs, sales scripts, or customer support FAQs, this is the material that should sit at the core of your AI knowledge base. A helpful trick: Search your inbox or Slack for the questions you're asked repeatedly. That's your goldmine.

2. **The integration phase:** Now that you've found your treasure trove of knowledge, it's time to plug it into the system—cleanly. This phase is where tech meets technique. Choose tools that are LLM friendly, meaning they can structure and surface data in a way the AI can parse—think platforms that support APIs, metadata tagging, and semantic search. Clear naming conventions and metadata standards are essential here (sorry, but "Final-Final-v2_UseThisOne.docx" doesn't cut it). Just as importantly, don't forget to train your team. Even the smartest AI needs well-fed inputs, and your people are the ones holding the spoon. Give them simple templates and play-books for how to capture new knowledge and where to store it. If it feels like extra work, make it fun: Give shoutouts or small rewards for great documentation. One team gave out gold star emoji and "Knowledge Ninja" badges—silly, yes, but it worked.

3. **The optimization phase:** Your knowledge base is live—now what? This is where the magic (and maintenance) happens. Start by reviewing usage analytics: what's being accessed, what's being ignored, and what's resulting in follow-up questions. This will tell you where your system is helping and where it's falling flat. Create feedback loops

so users can flag outdated info or suggest improvements, and don't let this fall into a black hole—act on the feedback. The best systems are living systems. You also want to keep knowledge flowing, so incentivize contributions. Recognize your internal knowledge heroes (yes, another badge won't hurt), bake knowledge capture into team processes, and set a recurring calendar reminder to review and refresh key areas. Think of it as flossing for your knowledge base—routine maintenance now prevents bigger issues later.

YOUR KNOWLEDGE EVOLUTION

Remember, implementing a modern knowledge base isn't just about organizing information—it's about getting into a mindset where learning and sharing become continuous and natural.

Your journey toward advanced knowledge management doesn't have to be perfect from day one. Start with the intelligence seed: a small, well-executed beginning that can grow into something remarkable. Remember, every great knowledge base starts with a single piece of information, properly stored and shared.

3

AI: The Ultimate Strategist, Mentor, and Coach

Sarah, our real estate broker, decided that her company needed to take things to the next level, so she started implementing basic AI coaching. "I began using Claude to analyze successful property listings and create guidelines for my team," she explained. "It was like having an experienced mentor available 24/7."

STARTING YOUR AI COACHING JOURNEY

In business and professional development, the transformative potential of AI is rapidly becoming a reality. Consider this: When Microsoft's CEO Satya Nadella announced that every employee would have an AI copilot, he wasn't just talking about complex coding assistants.

The company started with something surprisingly simple: using AI tools like Microsoft 365 Copilot to help employees improve their presentation skills and email communication. "Whether it's creating webinars, writing blogs, or responding to emails, AI has become an integral part of my daily communication tasks," shared Allison Michels, a senior program manager in the Microsoft Viva product group, in an article for Microsoft. This small AI intervention quickly proved powerful, helping employees communicate more clearly and efficiently across the organization, and setting the stage for broader AI adoption in their workflows.[1]

This was the first step of a crucial shift in learning and development: moving from periodic training to continuous improvement through AI.

LEARNING FROM EVERY INTERACTION

Instead of the traditional approach of quarterly training sessions, a start-up can use AI to extract insights from every customer interaction.

To illustrate this, here's an example of a prompt that can be used for customer support interaction analysis by providing the transcript of the call as an input.

> Please analyze:
> 1. Key moments that built customer trust
> 2. Effective problem-solving approaches used
> 3. Language choices that worked well
> 4. How the agent managed customer emotions
> 5. Specific techniques others can replicate

REAL-WORLD CASE STUDY
Unilever's AI-Powered FLEX Experiences

Unilever, the global consumer goods company, needed a way to keep its workforce agile while adapting to fast-changing business conditions. To address this, they launched FLEX Experiences, an AI-powered internal talent marketplace built with Gloat. The platform matches employees with short-term projects, mentorships, and full-time roles by analyzing their skills, experiences, and career aspirations.

The impact has been significant. Unilever redeployed more than 8,300 employees to business areas in need during the COVID-19 pandemic, unlocking capacity across the organization. Early users gave FLEX a 95 percent endorsement rate, highlighting how the platform helps employees grow their careers while meeting business needs. By turning transparency into opportunities and aligning talent with demand, FLEX has become a cornerstone of Unilever's workforce strategy.

This case demonstrates how AI-powered talent platforms can drive agility, employee engagement, and productivity in large organizations.[2]

THE PERFORMANCE AMPLIFICATION ZONE

What happens when AI coaching moves beyond basic skill development? This is where we enter the performance amplification zone—a state where AI and human expertise combine to create exponential excellence. According to research from MIT's Sloan School of Management, when highly skilled workers utilized AI tools for tasks within the AI's capabilities, their performance improved by nearly 40 percent compared to those who did not use AI.[3]

For example, a real estate agency could use Claude to analyze successful sales interactions and create a success playbook. To start, first upload a transcript of your agency's most successful property showing for a specific month. (Note: It's essential to obtain necessary permissions before recording and analyzing interactions.)

Then use the following prompt:

> Please analyze this interaction and:
> 1. Identify key moments that influenced the buyer.
> 2. Extract specific phrases and approaches that worked well.
> 3. Create a step-by-step guide for similar situations.
> 4. Suggest adaptations for different property types.
> 5. Draft sample responses for common objections.

The AI will then respond with key influential moments, effective phrases to use, and a step-by step approach to take. It's like having a master coach who can break down every success into teachable moments. Soon, you will build a library of proven approaches that will keep growing with every win.

PERPETUAL PERFORMANCE PEAKS

This leads us to one of the most fascinating patterns in AI coaching. Unlike traditional learning curves that tend to plateau, AI-enhanced skill development creates what I call Perpetual Performance Peaks—where each achievement becomes a launching pad for the next level of mastery.

PERPETUAL PERFORMANCE PEAKS IN AI INNOVATION

The concept of Perpetual Performance Peaks describes a continuous cycle of improvement, where each milestone serves as a foundation for reaching even greater heights.

This principle is particularly relevant to companies like OpenAI, where each AI model is not just a finished product but a stepping stone for the next breakthrough. By learning from prior models' limitations, successes, and user interactions, OpenAI refines its techniques, architectures, and training datasets to create more powerful and intelligent systems at an accelerating pace.

For example, GPT-3 laid the groundwork for GPT-4, which introduced better reasoning, reduced hallucinations, and improved contextual understanding. In turn, GPT-5 (and beyond) will leverage these advancements to push the boundaries of AI capabilities further.

This iterative process mirrors how high-performing athletes, businesses, and technologies achieve sustained success—analyzing performance, identifying weaknesses, and strategically improving with each cycle. In AI development, this means training models on larger datasets, refining architectures (such as transformer-based neural networks), and leveraging reinforcement learning from human feedback to enhance accuracy and safety.

OpenAI and competitors like Anthropic and Google DeepMind follow this "compounding intelligence" strategy, where innovation builds upon itself at an exponential rate. As a result, the time between significant AI advancements is shrinking, with each generation not just improving incrementally but often redefining what's possible. This continuous leapfrogging effect ensures that AI systems become smarter, more adaptable, and more aligned with human needs over time, embodying the essence of Perpetual Performance Peaks in artificial intelligence.

I have advised many teams to systematically capture and analyze client interactions to create growth journals. These journals can be used to identify patterns in client behavior, track team performance improvements, and develop data-driven strategies for enhancing service delivery. Growth journals serve as living repositories of insights that help teams understand what's working and what isn't, and they can show teams where opportunities for improvement exist. By consistently documenting client interactions, feedback, and outcomes, teams can spot trends early, replicate successful approaches, and proactively address emerging challenges before they become larger issues.

Here is an example of a prompt teams can use on a weekly basis to improve client relationships and service delivery:

Weekly Learning Analysis Prompt:

Here are our team's key client interactions from this week:

[Paste summaries]

Help us identify:

1. New successful approaches we should replicate
2. Emerging client concerns we need to address
3. Areas where we're improving
4. Opportunities for further enhancement
5. Specific wins to celebrate and learn from

The results will speak for themselves. Many teams I have worked with who have used prompts like this have maintained a consistent upward performance trajectory, with each quarter building upon the successes of the last.

Another example is Domino's Pizza's "DOM" AI/Voice Assistant. DOM functions as a voice-recognition ordering assistant. In early tests, it was used to take phoned-in carryout orders in a limited number of Domino's stores, alleviating workload from store staff so they could focus more on in-store customer service and order fulfillment.

DOM was introduced as part of Domino's broader digital and AI strategy, which includes integrating new AI tools with store operations, inventory management, and staff scheduling (through partnerships such as with Microsoft).[4]

This example shows how even a narrowly applied AI tool (voice ordering) can be part of a larger vision of embedding AI in operational workflows.

THE KNOWLEDGE TRANSFER NETWORK

One of the most powerful aspects of AI coaching is the ability to capture and distribute expertise across an entire organization. It is not just about technology—it's about creating the excellence echo effect, where every success creates ripples of improvement throughout the organization.

Even smaller organizations are achieving remarkable results through this approach. A regional insurance company implemented a simplified version using Microsoft Teams and AI analysis, improving knowledge-sharing effectiveness.

THE FUTURE OF AI COACHING

As we look ahead, we're entering an era where AI coaching doesn't just respond to current needs but anticipates future skill requirements. A McKinsey report discusses how integrating AI with human expertise can significantly enhance organizational performance. The report highlights the potential for significant productivity gains, stating that by 2030, up to 30 percent of current hours worked could be automated, accelerated by generative AI.[5]

This capability isn't limited to tech giants. A midsize marketing agency could use AI to analyze industry trends and client demands to shape their team development programs. This allows employees not to train just for today's needs but to prepare for changes before they become critical.

THE HUMAN ELEMENT: BEYOND DIGITAL COACHING

Perhaps the most potent realization in AI coaching is what is mentioned earlier in the book as what I call the Synergy Effect: understanding that AI enhances rather than replaces human capabilities. A study by Harvard Business School, conducted in collaboration with Boston Consulting Group, provides evidence supporting the Synergy Effect of AI enhancing human capabilities. In this study, consultants using AI tools completed 12.2 percent more tasks and did so 25.1 percent faster than those without AI assistance. Moreover, the quality of their work improved by over 40 percent.[6] These findings suggest that organizations emphasizing AI complementing human expertise can achieve higher adoption rates and significant performance gains.

This principle scales effectively across organizations of all sizes.

- **Small agency (three to five agents):** A boutique real estate firm might analyze their top three to five successful interactions monthly, creating a simple shared playbook. They could focus on their specific market niche—perhaps luxury condos or first-time homebuyers—and develop highly targeted approaches. The analysis might reveal that their most successful agent always mentions neighborhood coffee shops when showing properties to young professionals, leading to a standardized "lifestyle selling" approach for the entire team.

- **Midsize firm (twenty to fifty agents):** A regional agency analyzing interactions across different agent specialties and property types might discover that their commercial agents use completely different influence techniques than residential agents or that agents in urban markets have different success patterns than suburban specialists. This would lead to role-specific training materials and best practices that can be shared across similar positions company-wide.

- **Large enterprise (one hundred-plus agents across multiple markets):** A national real estate company could analyze thousands of interactions across different geographic markets, price points, and customer demographics. They might discover that successful approaches in Miami differ significantly from those in Minneapolis or that certain objection-handling techniques work universally while others are region specific. This creates a comprehensive knowledge system where agents can access best practices filtered by location, property type, client profile, and market conditions—essentially building an AI-powered success database that continuously learns from the organization's collective expertise.

Each level benefits from pattern recognition that would be impossible to identify manually. However, larger organizations gain exponentially more insights from their broader datasets, while smaller firms benefit from highly focused, actionable guidance tailored to their specific market niche.

PREPARING FOR YOUR AI COACHING JOURNEY

As we conclude this chapter, remember that the real power isn't in the technology; it's in how the technology helps us understand and develop our human potential. Implementing AI coaching isn't about becoming more automated; it's about becoming more authentic in how you grow and learn. The key is starting with the foundation focus, identifying where AI can provide immediate value while building toward more sophisticated applications. Whether you're a global enterprise or a growing team, the principles remain the same: Use AI to enhance human potential, not replace it.

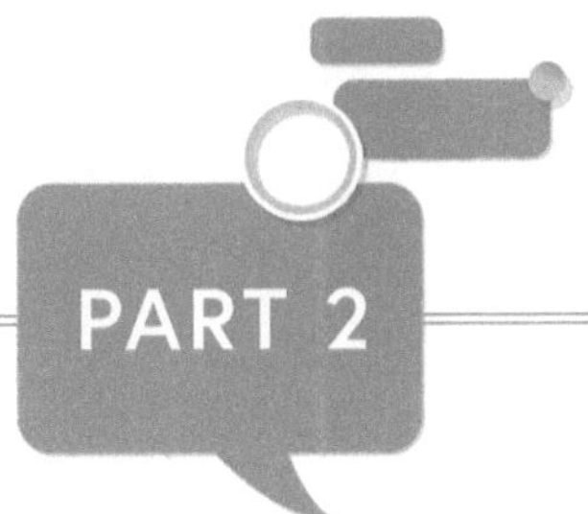

COACHING IN SALES:

HOW AI TRANSFORMS SALES PROFESSIONALS

4

AI, The Ultimate Rainmaker: Supercharging Prospecting and Lead Generation

When Dropbox's sales team faced the challenge of identifying and engaging enterprise prospects at scale, they ventured into intelligent prospecting. The core issue wasn't finding leads—it was quickly accessing scattered prospect information across multiple systems when engaging with hot leads. Sales reps were losing valuable response time hunting through CRMs, email threads, case studies, and research tools to piece together the complete prospect picture before reaching out.

To resolve this pain point, Dropbox introduced Dropbox Dash, an AI-powered universal search tool designed to centralize information across workplace applications. Dash enables users to locate, organize, and act on content seamlessly, regardless of where it resides. So when a warm lead comes in, sales reps can instantly surface all relevant prospect intelligence— from industry-specific case studies to pricing proposals—allowing them to respond with personalized, compelling outreach while the lead is still hot, dramatically improving conversion rates.

Unlike generic AI chatbots, Dash leverages machine learning to continuously improve its results, adapting to user behavior and needs over time. Its generative AI capabilities also allow users to ask complex queries and receive synthesized relevant insights.[1]

Both Sarah and Michael could benefit from this kind of prospecting technology. Sarah stared at her monitor, surrounded by browser tabs full of potential leads that felt about as organized as a teenager's bedroom. "I knew there was valuable information in there somewhere," she recalled with a laugh.

Michael faced his own prospecting puzzle. His loan officers were spending more time sifting through leads than actually helping clients. "We were drowning in data but thirsty for insights," he shared. "It was like having a library full of books but no idea which books were worth reading and which ones to read first."

This challenge is precisely why AI-powered prospecting tools have become essential for modern sales teams.

THE NEW INTELLIGENCE:
AI-POWERED PROSPECTING TOOLS

Before we dive into strategies, let's look at the tools reshaping the prospecting landscape.

VOICE AI ASSISTANTS: THE NEW TEAM MEMBERS

The integration of Voice AI in prospecting is helping organizations use every interaction as a source of insights for future engagements. These systems can handle basic qualification questions, schedule meetings, address common objections, route calls to appropriate team members, and transcribe and analyze conversations.

For businesses not ready for enterprise-level Voice AI, several accessible options exist.

Entry-Level Voice AI Solutions

- **Otter.ai and ChatGPT:** Record calls, generate transcripts, analyze patterns
- **Rev and Claude:** Transcription with detailed conversation analysis
- **Fireflies.ai:** AI meeting assistant with basic pattern recognition

Mid-Level Solutions

- **Gong.io:** Conversation intelligence and coaching
- **Chorus.ai:** Call recording and AI-powered insights
- **RingCentral AI:** Integrated communications with AI analysis

Enterprise solutions like Gong.io and Chorus.ai (recently acquired by ZoomInfo) have transformed how large organizations handle calls. For smaller teams, tools like Otter.ai combined with ChatGPT provide a practical starting point. "We record our calls with Otter, then use ChatGPT to analyze the transcripts," Sarah explained.

"We started with basic call recording and transcription," Michael shared. "Even that simple setup helped us identify patterns we were missing."

LARGE LANGUAGE MODELS (LLM): YOUR PROSPECTING PARTNERS

Different LLMs excel at varying aspects of prospecting. For example, ChatGPT is excellent for crafting personalized outreach messages. Claude is superior at analyzing complex market data and client patterns, and Gemini is strong at multimodal analysis, which is great for property photos and descriptions. GPT-5 is the best option for sophisticated strategy development and market analysis.

REAL-WORLD CASE STUDY
Cognism's AI Search

Cognism, an AI-powered sales intelligence platform, demonstrates the power of AI in prospecting. Using its "AI Search" functionality, Cognism enables sales teams to identify high-value leads faster than ever before. For instance, sales reps can type commands like "Find companies with over 500 employees using Marketo" into the search bar. Then the AI will instantly generate a list of qualified leads based on the specified criteria.

The results have been transformative. There was a 74 percent reduction in prospecting time. Sales teams identify their total addressable market three times faster. Lead conversion rates improved due to better targeting.

Cognism's approach highlights how AI can eliminate manual research and focus sales efforts on the most promising opportunities.[2]

THE LEAD INTELLIGENCE MATRIX

What sets modern prospecting apart is identifying who might be interested and when they're most likely to engage. HubSpot's AI system analyzes over one hundred behavioral signals to predict purchase intent with remarkable accuracy, enabling sales teams to identify who might be interested in their products and when they're most likely to engage.[3]

For smaller operations, this level of insight is still achievable through the clever use of available tools. For example, a lending team could use a combination of LinkedIn Sales Navigator and ChatGPT to analyze potential clients. Here's an example of what a prompt and ChatGPT response could look like:

> Here's the LinkedIn activity and website behavior of a potential client:
>
> [Paste data]
>
> Please analyze:
> 1. Signals indicating loan readiness
> 2. Potential pain points to address
> 3. Optimal timing for outreach
> 4. Personalization opportunities
> 5. Relevant case studies to reference

Loan Readiness Signals:
- Recent LinkedIn posts about business expansion and hiring suggest capital needs
- Website visits to equipment financing pages indicate specific loan interest
- Engagement with industry growth content shows forward-thinking mindset

Pain Points to Address:
- Cash flow concerns evident from posts about delayed client payments
- Equipment upgrade needs based on competitor comparison research
- Seasonal revenue fluctuations mentioned in recent company updates

Optimal Timing:

- Reach out within next 2 weeks while expansion planning is active
- Best contact time appears to be Tuesday–Thursday mornings based on posting patterns
- Avoid month-end when they seem focused on collections

Personalization Opportunities:

- Reference their recent trade show participation in manufacturing expo
- Mention shared connection with ABC Company (visible in their network)
- Acknowledge their sustainability initiatives mentioned in recent posts

Relevant Case Studies:

- Similar manufacturing client who used equipment financing for expansion
- Case study about seasonal businesses managing cash flow with credit lines

As you can see, AI transformed raw prospect data into actionable outreach intelligence that Michael can use immediately.

THE DIGITAL BODY LANGUAGE DECODER

One of the most powerful aspects of AI-powered prospecting is what I term the Digital Body Language Decoder: the ability to understand prospects' intentions through their online behavior patterns. Microsoft's sales team uses advanced machine learning to analyze thousands of digital touchpoints, helping them predict with significantly improved accuracy when a company is ready to make a purchase decision.[4]

But you don't need Microsoft's resources to implement this concept— you can achieve success with a simpler approach. A real estate team could use ChatGPT to analyze property viewing patterns on its website if they noticed that serious buyers had specific behavioral patterns. For example, some buyers looked at property taxes, school districts, and commute times all in one session. The AI could help them to spot those patterns and reach out at just the right moment.

Instead of one user at a time, if you want to understand what *all* your users want, care about, and interact with on your site by visually representing their clicks, taps, and scrolling behavior, heatmap analytics help you find that. According to Hotjar, heatmaps are one of the services you can install on your website for such analytics. "Heatmaps give you an aggregate of engagement across your website pages and can be split by clicks, taps, and scrolling behavior—allowing you to quickly see things like the average drop-off point on your blog posts or what your users expected to be clickable during checkout."[5]

THE PROSPECT JOURNEY MAPPER

What truly sets modern prospecting apart is the ability to understand and map a prospect's journey before they even reach out. Here's how a real estate agency can adapt this concept.

Prospect Journey Analysis Prompt

Here's a potential buyer's website activity over the past month:

[Paste activity log]

Please help me:

1. Map their property preferences
2. Identify their likely time frame
3. Spot potential concerns

> 4. Suggest personalized outreach
> 5. Recommend relevant properties

Though the patterns that may emerge could be exciting and have the potential to be a big sale, you have to be realistic. Just because someone looked at luxury penthouses for three hours doesn't mean they're a qualified buyer; sometimes people just enjoy virtual window-shopping.

THE AUTOMATION INTELLIGENCE NETWORK

AI is changing how organizations handle lead nurturing at scale. For smaller teams, this level of sophistication is achievable through a clever combination of available tools. Here's how a midsize consulting firm can structure their approach:

1. **Initial contact:** Use GPT-5 for personalized outreach.

2. **Follow-up:** Leverage Claude for response analysis.

3. **Meeting scheduling:** Use Calendly with custom rules.

4. **Content sharing:** Create personalized content recommendations via ChatGPT.

5. **Engagement tracking:** Build simple analytics combined with AI insight.

THE PREDICTIVE PIPELINE PROTOCOL

One of the most powerful developments in AI-powered prospecting is the ability to predict not just who might buy but when they're most likely to do so.

In order to make predictions regarding who might buy a specific product or service, the AI looks at historical buying patterns, digital body language, and company growth indicators. The AI also analyzes current market conditions and economic trends in order to determine the timing of such purchases.

A lender could use a combination of public data and AI analysis to predict loan demand. If a lender tracks building permits, home listings, and local business expansion news, then feeds that into an AI analysis, they can get a pretty good picture of where the market's heading.

REAL-WORLD CASE STUDY

Microsoft's Predictive Lead Scoring in Dynamics 365

Microsoft embedded predictive lead scoring into its Dynamics 365 Sales platform as part of the Sales Insights suite. The AI model analyzes factors such as demographics (e.g., industry or role), behavioral signals (e.g., email opens or event participation), and historical data (e.g., past purchases) to prioritize leads more likely to convert.

The system highlights the top influencing factors for each score, giving sales teams visibility into *why* a lead is ranked highly and allowing administrators to refine models over time. By focusing on high-scoring leads, organizations can reduce time spent on low-quality opportunities and improve alignment between marketing and sales teams.[6]

THE PERSONAL TOUCH PARADOX

Another surprising discovery in AI-powered prospecting is the counterintuitive truth that using AI can actually make your outreach more personal, not less. According to a 2024 article from Vena Solutions, 16 percent of sales professionals use generative AI for prospect outreach, indicating a growing trend in leveraging AI for personalized communication.[7]

Adobe uses AI to create "Real Time Customer Profiles" by combining data from multiple sources to deliver personalized experiences. Real-Time Customer Profile operates as a comprehensive data unification system that ingests information from multiple touchpoints, including website behavior, offline purchases, CRM systems, and third-party sources, then uses an identity graph to stitch together all customer identifiers into unified profiles. The system applies merge policies to resolve data conflicts, employs machine learning through features like Customer AI to generate behavioral predictions such as churn likelihood or conversion probability, and ultimately enables real-time audience segmentation for personalized, coordinated marketing experiences across all channels.[8]

THE MULTICHANNEL MASTERY MATRIX

Modern prospecting isn't just about reaching out—it's a strategy optimized through omnichannel omnipresence. Google's B2B division demonstrates this through its sophisticated multichannel approach, using AI to coordinate outreach across email, social media, content marketing, and direct contact.

For smaller organizations, this level of coordination is achievable through the strategic orchestration of readily available tools, creating a unified customer intelligence system without enterprise-level budgets. A regional insurance agency can use this approach by weaving together multiple AI-enhanced platforms to create seamless prospect engagement workflows. They can begin with LinkedIn Sales Navigator to identify potential clients based on life events, career changes, or business milestones that indicate insurance needs, then feed this prospect data into ChatGPT, where agents can generate highly personalized outreach messages that references specific details from the prospect's professional background or recent achievements.

Hootsuite's AI enhancement features can optimize the timing and frequency of social media touchpoints, ensuring the agency maintains visibility without overwhelming prospects. Meanwhile, their email automation system delivers follow-up sequences at optimal engagement times, while Voice AI handles initial contact screening to qualify leads before they reach human agents.[9] This integrated approach transforms what could be a disjointed collection of tools into a cohesive customer intelligence ecosystem. The result is a level of personalization and coordination that rivals much larger competitors, demonstrating how smaller organizations can leverage AI integration to punch above their weight class in customer engagement and conversion rates.

THE ETHICS OF AI PROSPECTING: NAVIGATING THE FINE LINE BETWEEN INNOVATION AND RESPONSIBILITY

With great power comes great responsibility, and nowhere is this more true than in AI-powered prospecting. The trust–tech balance has become crucial as organizations navigate the line between personalization and privacy.

In Johann Wolfgang von Goethe's 1797 poem "The Sorcerer's Apprentice," an eager apprentice, left alone by his master, attempts to use magic to animate a broom to fetch water. At first, the broom obediently follows the apprentice's commands, but soon things spiral out of control as the broom floods the workshop. Lacking the knowledge to undo the spell, the apprentice is helpless as the situation escalates. This timeless tale warns of unleashing powerful forces without proper oversight, which can lead to unintended and potentially disastrous consequences.

Fast forward to today, where AI-driven prospecting in sales and marketing bears striking similarities to the sorcerer's broom. AI can automate tasks, identify potential customers, and personalize outreach at scale—but if not managed properly, it can create serious ethical challenges. From biased algorithms to data privacy concerns, businesses must ensure that AI remains a tool for enhanced decision-making rather than an unchecked force that leads to reputational damage and regulatory scrutiny.

THE ETHICAL PITFALLS OF AI IN PROSPECTING

AI-powered prospecting is an incredible asset for sales teams, allowing them to identify high-value leads, analyze customer behavior, and automate outreach. However, when deployed irresponsibly, AI can introduce serious risks.

Algorithmic Bias: When AI Becomes an Unintended Gatekeeper

AI is only as good as the data it's trained on. If the data contains historical biases, AI can reinforce and amplify them—often without businesses even realizing it.

One of the most infamous examples of AI bias in decision-making comes from Amazon's AI-powered hiring tool. In 2014, Amazon developed an AI model to streamline its recruiting process. However, the system favored male candidates over female applicants because it was trained on historical hiring data, which was predominantly male. As a result, the AI downgraded resumes that included the word "women's," such as "women's chess club captain," leading to a biased hiring process.[10]

A biased AI system used for lead generation could inadvertently filter out minority-owned businesses, female executives, or clients in certain geographic regions based on historical sales data. Without human oversight, sales teams may unknowingly miss out on diverse, high-potential prospects.

In order to prevent this, teams must regularly audit AI prospecting tools to ensure fairness. Teams may need to implement transparency measures, such as requiring explainable AI outputs that show why specific prospects were prioritized or filtered out, and use AI models designed to actively mitigate bias, such as fairness-aware algorithms that deliberately include diverse prospect pools and weight demographic factors to prevent historical exclusion patterns from perpetuating.

Data Privacy Concerns: When AI Knows Too Much

AI prospecting relies on large amounts of customer data to predict buying behavior and identify high-potential leads. But where do we draw the line between insightful and intrusive?

One notorious case of AI overstepping privacy boundaries was Target's predictive analytics model, which accurately determined that a teenage girl was pregnant before her father knew. Target used AI to analyze purchasing behaviors, such as buying unscented lotion and supplements, to predict pregnancy stages. They then sent pregnancy-related advertisements to the teenager's home, leading to a privacy breach that sparked controversy.[11]

Companies that use AI for sales prospecting must take steps to not collect and use personal data in ways that make customers uncomfortable. If a prospect receives an outreach email that too precisely anticipates their needs, they might feel violated rather than engaged.

Following a privacy-first AI approach is a step in the right direction. Companies can show their consumers that they care about their privacy by complying with customer data protection laws, such as GDPR and

CCPA, and providing transparency on how AI makes prospecting decisions. Companies should also limit AI to aggregating data, not personal information.

The key to ethical AI prospecting lies in balancing personalization with privacy—a balance that protects both customers and business relationships. Companies prioritizing transparency and consent build deeper trust with prospects who appreciate knowing how their data is used, leading to more positive engagement and long-term partnerships. The most successful AI prospecting strategies recognize that sustainable growth comes from earning customer trust, not exploiting data advantages. By implementing privacy-first approaches with human oversight, organizations can harness intelligent prospecting while preserving the ethical foundation of successful business.

Companies That Are Getting AI Prospecting Right

While some companies have faced challenges with AI-driven decision-making, others have set a gold standard for ethical AI implementation in prospecting and customer engagement.

Apple has built its AI ecosystem with privacy as a foundational principle; unlike other tech giants that rely on cloud-based data storage for AI training, Apple processes much of its AI computations directly on users' devices. This ensures that personal data remains private while still allowing AI to provide intelligent recommendations.[12]

Apple also employs differential privacy, which adds random noise—intentionally introducing small, random changes to individual data points—to user data before it is analyzed, making it impossible to identify any single person's information while still allowing useful patterns to emerge from the overall dataset.[13] Sales teams can adopt Apple's privacy-first approach by ensuring AI prospecting tools do not track personally identifiable information unnecessarily. They can also allow prospects to control how much data is shared.

IBM has also taken a proactive stance on responsible AI. They established guiding principles that emphasize explainability (understanding how AI makes decisions), fairness and bias mitigation, and transparency in AI operations. These ethical guardrails are designed to prevent misuse, and the company actively collaborates with regulators to ensure compliance with emerging AI laws.[14]

IBM's model demonstrates the importance of explainability in AI prospecting. Sales teams should ensure that prospects understand why they were targeted and that AI recommendations are clear and traceable.

AI PROSPECTING AS A FORCE FOR GOOD

"The Sorcerer's Apprentice" reminds us that powerful technology must be carefully controlled to prevent unintended consequences. AI in sales prospecting has the potential to revolutionize efficiency and personalization, but without ethical oversight, it can harm reputations, violate privacy, and introduce bias.

By learning from past mistakes (Amazon, Target) and emulating best practices (Apple, IBM), companies can ensure that AI prospecting is fair, transparent, and privacy conscious. With the right balance of innovation and responsibility, AI can remain a powerful sales ally rather than an out-of-control spell gone wrong.

For smaller organizations, maintaining this balance is equally important. Michael's team developed their own ethical guidelines. "We use the Grandmother Test," he explained. "If you wouldn't be comfortable with your grandmother knowing how you got the information, don't use it in prospecting."

To ensure AI prospecting enhances sales efficiency without crossing ethical boundaries, companies should follow these best practices:

- **Transparency in AI decisions:** Ensure sales reps and customers understand why AI is recommending a certain lead or prioritizing a prospect.

- **Bias audits:** Regularly audit AI-prospecting models to detect and correct biases that may exclude valuable prospects.

- **Privacy-first AI approaches:** Follow Apple's example—use on-device processing where possible and anonymize data for insights.

- **Customer consent and control:** Allow customers to opt out of AI-driven targeting and provide control over how their data is used.

- **Human oversight is key:** AI should enhance, not replace, human judgment, and sales teams should always have the final say in prospecting decisions.

As we've seen throughout this chapter, AI has fundamentally transformed prospecting from an art of persistence to a science of precision. From identifying high-value prospects to engaging them at the perfect moment, AI tools enable sales teams of all sizes to work smarter. By streamlining knowledge retrieval, AI-powered search solutions, like the Dropbox Dash we talked about earlier in the chapter, don't just boost efficiency—they fundamentally reshape modern workflows, freeing professionals from time-consuming searches and allowing them to focus on high-impact tasks.

Whether you're a large enterprise like Microsoft or a small team like Sarah's, the principles remain the same: Start with a clear understanding of your needs, implement tools thoughtfully, and always balance technical capabilities with human judgment.

5

From Rookie to Rock Star: AI-Driven Sales Role-Playing

Sarah was trying not to laugh while watching one of her newer agents attempting to smooth-talk their way through a simulated luxury property showing. The AI had decided to play the role of an eccentric tech billionaire who insisted on knowing if the wine cellar could be converted into a personal cryogenic freezing chamber and whether the home's Wi-Fi could support their cryptocurrency mining operation. The agent, to their credit, was maintaining remarkable composure.

These moments of AI-induced hilarity aside, Sarah and her team were experiencing the reality that practice doesn't make perfect; practice makes permanent.

"Practice makes permanent" highlights a critical truth: Repetition alone does not lead to mastery. When practice occurs without proper guidance or feedback, it can entrench ineffective habits and flawed decision-making. Over time, these patterns become deeply ingrained, making them difficult to reverse and ultimately limiting performance. Rather than driving continuous improvement, unguided practice can solidify mediocrity and hinder the pursuit of excellence.

Enter AI-powered role-playing. This isn't your typical script reading or awkward peer-to-peer practice; it's what happens when artificial intelligence creates practice spaces that adapt and respond in real time to your performance.

USING AI FOR ROLE-PLAYING: A GAME CHANGER FOR SALES PROFESSIONALS

One of the most powerful capabilities of LLMs like ChatGPT is role prompting, where AI takes on specific personas to simulate real-life conversations. For sales professionals, this means they can practice pitches, handle objections, and refine their negotiation skills by engaging in dynamic, interactive role-play with AI. Unlike traditional training methods, AI role-playing is available on demand and can adapt in real time, providing customized scenarios based on the salesperson's industry, product, or skill level.

For example, imagine an AI that notices a salesperson using too many filler words and gradually increases interruptions from the simulated customer whenever this behavior appears. This allows for low-risk, high-impact practice sessions, where mistakes become learning opportunities without real-world consequences.

Structured Role-Playing Prompts

- **Basic scenario:** Pretend you are a first-time homebuyer concerned about mortgage rates. Ask me questions, and I'll try to address your concerns.

- **Intermediate challenge:** You are a skeptical CFO considering our software, but you think it's too expensive. Challenge me with tough financial objections, and I will try to convince you otherwise.

- **Advanced negotiation:** Act as a competitor's customer hesitant to switch to our product. Let's have a detailed conversation where I try to win your business.

By iterating on these conversations and analyzing AI's feedback, sales professionals can identify communication gaps, refine persuasion techniques, and build confidence in handling real-world objections. The ability to simulate different customer personas and resistance levels makes AI role-playing an essential tool for sales training, allowing professionals to sharpen their skills in a structured yet flexible environment.

CoachAI, an AI coaching platform that I created in 2023, helps sales professionals in multiple industries role-play with various client personas created for their specific needs. The master coach, "Zig," further enhances a user's sales skill by coaching on techniques, strategies, and new ideas to help them upskill and improve their performance.

THE REALITY BRIDGE

"The first time I tried it, I was skeptical," one real estate agent who used CoachAI admitted. "I thought, *How realistic can this be?* Then the AI threw a curveball at me—asking about the property's resale potential given the new highway construction planned three miles away and whether the school district boundaries might change in the next five years—questions that were so specific and realistic, so precisely what my most thorough clients would research and ask, I actually felt the same pressure I do in real showings. That's when I realized how valuable this system was."

The breakthrough came when agents discovered the AI's ability to simulate diverse client concerns and objection patterns. "We have clients with completely different priorities and knowledge levels," the agent explained.

"The AI can switch from a first-time buyer worried about maintenance costs to an experienced investor questioning neighborhood appreciation trends and rental yield potential, helping our agents practice handling the full spectrum of realistic scenarios they encounter daily."

THE INTELLIGENCE IMMERSION EFFECT

The power of these simulations lies in their ability to create a safe growth zone—where professionals can push their boundaries without real-world consequences. The AI records every practice session, analyzing not just words but subtle nuances in tone and pacing.

"It's like having a dozen different clients to practice with," one real estate agent explained, "but without the risk of losing any of them." This agent had recently survived what the team now jokingly calls "*The Great British Bake Off* Incident," where the AI role-played a client who insisted on evaluating kitchen spaces by pretending to host an imaginary cooking show. Though amusing, the exercise led to valuable insights about showcasing kitchen functionality.

This fictional, yet unexpected scenario, also highlights the importance of engaging storytelling in property tours. As a result, the real estate teams can incorporate more narrative-driven demonstrations, emphasizing how kitchen spaces could support different lifestyles, from hosting dinner parties to being a functional workspace for home chefs.

TRANSFORMING COACHING WITH AI: THE KORN FERRY AND YOODLI STORY

Korn Ferry, a global leader in organizational consulting, supports companies in hiring, leadership development, and workforce motivation.

While their Talent Suite platform provided access to certified coaches and learning content, they needed a more scalable way to reinforce coaching sessions. To address these challenges, a case study presented by Yoodli, titled "How Korn Ferry Transformed Their Coaching Offering Using Yoodli AI Communication Coach," shows how Korn Ferry integrated an AI-powered communication coach into their Talent Suite.

THE CHALLENGE: SCALING AND ENHANCING COACHING REINFORCEMENT

The leadership team identified three key pain points:

1. **Scalability:** Existing digital content lacked interactive practice opportunities.

2. **Expanded communication coaching:** Their platform only offered basic interview prep feedback, missing broader business conversations.

3. **Speed and cost efficiency:** Building an AI-powered solution internally would be expensive and time consuming.[1]

THE SOLUTION: AI-DRIVEN ROLE-PLAY AND REAL-TIME FEEDBACK

Yoodli allowed users to practice conversations—from job interviews and sales pitches to difficult workplace discussions—while receiving instant AI-driven feedback based on Korn Ferry's proprietary coaching methodology. Yoodli's real-time analytics helped quantify speaking patterns, enabling coaches to focus on high-level coaching rather than mechanical speech corrections.[2]

By embedding Yoodli within the platform, Korn Ferry maintained full data security compliance (SOC 2, GDPR), ensuring that practice sessions remained confidential. The AI coaching tool was positioned as a valuable reinforcement aid, with almost all Korn Ferry coaches recommending it to clients.

THE IMPACT: FASTER ADOPTION AND COMPETITIVE EDGE

- **Rapid deployment:** AI coaching was integrated in under a month, significantly faster than developing in-house.

- **Cost savings:** Korn Ferry saved on labor, development, and storage costs.

- **Competitive differentiation:** Yoodli-powered coaching is now a standard offering in client pitches and RFPs.

- **Enhanced client experience:** Clients found the AI role-play challenging yet effective, making practice sessions more engaging.[3]

This seamless AI–human coaching partnership has given Korn Ferry a market advantage, making coaching reinforcement more accessible, data driven, and impactful.

THE FEEDBACK REVOLUTION

The true power of AI role-playing lies in the instant insight loop—feedback that's not just immediate but intelligently layered. Here's an example of a prompt a real estate team can use to implement the role-playing AI:

Role: Create a simulation for a luxury property presentation

Scenario: $4.2 million beachfront property with unique architectural features

Client profile: Tech executive, detail-oriented, concerned about privacy

Key Challenges:

- Highlighting smart-home integration
- Addressing security concerns
- Explaining unique architectural elements
- Handling objections about price per square foot

Feedback Focus:

- Technical knowledge accuracy
- Confidence in presentation
- Response to specific objections

The AI would then create dynamic scenarios where agents could practice presenting high-end properties while receiving real-time feedback on their performance. The AI will also adapt its responses based on the agent's confidence level with technical details. So if someone struggled with explaining the smart-home features, the AI would ask increasingly more specific questions until that weakness was identified and addressed. Essentially, the AI doesn't just play the role of the client—it actively coaches during the simulation.

Many AI simulators do this. Every individual or salesperson who uses CoachAI starts with a "neutral" rating. But with every answer the salesperson gives to a question, the rating turns to *bad* if the answer is not satisfactory, moves to *good* if the answer is as good or better than expected, or simply stays neutral if the answer is adequate. This "instant insight" gives the salesperson feedback that they can easily and quickly incorporate to achieve the desired result instead of waiting for feedback after thirty minutes of role-playing, when it's too late to go back and make course corrections.

THE PRESSURE PERFORMANCE PROTOCOL

One of the most fascinating aspects of AI role-playing that we implemented in CoachAI is the Pressure Performance Protocol: the ability to gradually increase scenario complexity and stakes. This ensures that the salesperson skill is never stagnated and continuously evolving to a greater height.

The following is an example prompt for a progressive challenge system:

> Session type: Progressive challenge simulation
>
> Base scenario: Luxury property showing
>
> Progressive elements:
> 1. Standard showing (baseline)
> 2. Add difficult questions about market conditions
> 3. Introduce competing property comparisons
> 4. Add time pressure element
> 5. Include multiple decision-makers with conflicting priorities

This progressive challenge system transforms theoretical training into practical mastery by building complexity layer by layer. Real estate agents report that by the time they complete all five levels, they've developed the confidence and skills to handle even the most demanding luxury clients. The system's effectiveness lies in its graduated approach: Agents master each skill set before adding new challenges, preventing overwhelm while ensuring they're genuinely prepared for the unpredictable nature of high-stakes property transactions. Most importantly, agents find that after completing these progressive simulations, real client interactions feel more manageable because they've already navigated similar scenarios in a controlled environment where mistakes become learning opportunities rather than lost deals.

THE MICRO-MOMENT MASTERY MODEL

Micro-moments are those fleeting yet pivotal interactions where split-second decisions and reactions can dramatically alter outcomes. I developed the Micro-Moment Model, which focuses on identifying and optimizing the countless small moments that collectively create exceptional performance. For example, a 2022 Harvard Business Review study found that managers who consistently engage in micro-behaviors such as empathy and recognition see marked increases in team engagement and trust. These micro-moments contribute to building psychological safety, resilience, and sustained collaboration over time, going beyond broad skill gaps to explain differences in performance levels.[4]

These micro-moments can manifest in a myriad of scenarios across various professional domains. In sales, a well-timed and expertly crafted rebuttal to an objection can be the difference between closing a deal and losing a potential client. In customer service, an empathetic and understanding acknowledgment of a customer's concern can de-escalate a tense situation and foster loyalty. During high-stakes negotiations, a subtle yet precise adjustment in phrasing can sway the balance of power and lead to a more favorable agreement.

AI-powered coaching has ushered in a new era of leveraging these micro-moments for continuous improvement and enhanced performance. By meticulously analyzing vast amounts of data from customer interactions, sales calls, and other communication channels, AI algorithms can identify patterns and trends that would be impossible for humans to discern. These insights can then be used to develop personalized coaching strategies that target specific areas for improvement.

For example, AI can analyze the language and tone used in successful sales calls to identify the key phrases and communication styles that resonate most with customers. This information can then be used to coach sales representatives on how to improve their pitch and increase their close rate. Similarly, AI can analyze customer service interactions to identify the most effective ways to handle complaints and resolve issues. This information can then be used to coach customer service representatives on how to provide better support and improve customer satisfaction.

While negotiating, AI can analyze the strategies and tactics used by successful negotiators to identify the most effective ways to influence outcomes. This information can then be used to coach negotiators on how to improve their bargaining skills and achieve their desired results.

Overall, the ability to harness the power of micro-moments through AI-powered coaching has the potential to revolutionize the way we communicate and interact in professional settings. By providing targeted and personalized feedback, AI can help individuals and organizations alike to unlock their full potential and achieve greater success.

Micro-moment strategies are widely used across tourism and leisure brands. One notable example is Oracle's work with Disneyland Paris. In this case, Oracle employed contextual intelligence—an AI-driven approach that interprets real-time behavior, location, and browsing activity—to place ads that were not only targeted to the right audience but delivered at moments when they would be most meaningful. This ensured the messaging felt timely, relevant, and aligned with what users were experiencing or looking for in that moment.

For example, families browsing European vacation destinations would see magical Disneyland Paris content featuring popular characters and attractions, while users searching for weekend activities near Paris received targeted promotions for day passes and special events.[5]

THE IMPLEMENTATION BLUEPRINT: NAVIGATING CHALLENGES

As powerful as AI role-playing can be, success depends on a systematic approach to implementation that anticipates and addresses common challenges.

TECHNICAL INTEGRATION HURDLES: THE LEARNING CURVE

When rolling out an AI role-playing program, you might discover that technical hurdles aren't just about system compatibility—they are also about human adaptability. Veteran agents who had mastered traditional client interactions may find themselves fumbling with basic interface controls, while younger team members race ahead with the technology but miss crucial professional nuances. The solution? Buddy teams, pairing tech-savvy team members with experienced professionals.

Numerous organizations have found that peer-to-peer support dramatically accelerates adoption rates.

OVERCOMING RESISTANCE: FROM SKEPTICS TO BELIEVERS

The introduction of AI role-playing simulations often encounters resistance rooted in legitimate professional concerns. Experienced team members may perceive these tools as a fundamental challenge to their accumulated expertise and professional identity—a mechanization of the nuanced human judgment they've spent years developing.

Yet skepticism often masks valuable institutional knowledge. Those who resist most strongly frequently possess the deepest understanding of contextual complexities that pure AI solutions might overlook. The path forward: Engage skeptics as cocreators in scenario design, leveraging their expertise to identify the subtle dynamics and edge cases that make simulations truly valuable.

When positioned correctly, AI becomes a tool for preserving, scaling, and transmitting the tacit knowledge that experienced professionals have accumulated, ensuring that expertise enhances rather than constrains organizational capability.

THE CALIBRATION CONUNDRUM: FINDING THE SWEET SPOT

One of the most critical yet overlooked aspects of AI role-playing implementation is calibrating the difficulty level to match your team's current capabilities and growth trajectory. Get this balance wrong and you'll either overwhelm your people into avoidance or bore them into disengagement.

The key insight from early implementations is that scenarios that prove too challenging, even for experienced team members, signal a need for recalibration. Conversely, scenarios that fail to engage indicate insufficient challenge. The solution lies in applying principles from video game design, particularly dynamic difficulty adjustment. Successful AI role-playing implementations now adjust their challenge levels based on user performance and confidence indicators.

This adaptive approach involves programming AI systems to detect subtle signs of confidence or stress in participants' responses during simulations. When these indicators are recognized, the AI automatically adjusts the scenario complexity to maintain what psychologists call the "zone of proximal development"—that sweet spot between what a learner can do independently and what they can achieve with support from someone more skilled.[6] This ensures that participants are challenged but not overwhelmed.

ENGAGEMENT EVOLUTION: KEEPING IT FRESH

When teams experience simulation fatigue after extended exposure to AI role-playing programs, even enthusiastic participants begin treating exercises as routine.

The solution: "Plot Twist Tuesdays"—a methodology where AI introduces unexpected elements into standard scenarios. Imagine a routine client meeting simulation where the AI suddenly plays a colleague handling a crisis while insisting the meeting continue. The participant must maintain focus and professionalism despite the chaos.

These unexpected variations transform routine practice into dynamic learning experiences that mirror real-world unpredictability while maintaining engagement through novelty.

REAL-WORLD CASE STUDY

Ergeon Inc.'s AI-Powered Onboarding Success

Ergeon Inc., a construction technology start-up, faced challenges in scaling their sales training program. They implemented SellMeThis-Pen (SMTP), an AI-driven sales coaching platform, to train forty-seven boot camp attendees simultaneously. The results were impressive:

- 90 percent onboarding graduation rate for new hires

continued

> • Significant reduction in leadership time spent on training
> • Ability to scale training without compromising quality
>
> Ergeon's director of sales noted that the AI tool aligned perfectly with their values of investing in people and staying lean.[7]

TAKING ROLE-PLAYING TO THE NEXT LEVEL

The integration of virtual reality (VR) and augmented reality (AR) can revolutionize role-playing for sales professionals by creating immersive, real-world training environments that enhance skill development far beyond traditional AI-based text simulations. Unlike conventional role-playing with AI chatbots, VR and AR can provide realistic face-to-face interactions, body language cues, and contextual elements that mimic real-world sales scenarios.

Some companies are already experimenting with VR sales training platforms that allow professionals to practice pitches, objections, and negotiations in a fully immersive 3D setting, for example:

- **Virtual sales meetings:** A sales rep puts on a VR headset and enters a simulated boardroom where they must pitch their product to a panel of lifelike avatars representing skeptical executives. The AI-powered avatars react dynamically based on tone, content, and persuasion techniques, forcing the salesperson to adjust their approach in real time.

- **Trade show and retail training:** Using AR glasses (like Microsoft HoloLens), a retail associate can see virtual customers walking into a store and interact with them as they navigate product displays. AI-driven customers might ask questions, hesitate, or show buying signals, allowing the trainee to practice engagement strategies in a controlled, data-driven environment.

- **High-stakes negotiation simulations:** A VR-powered role-play can place sales professionals in a stressful, high-pressure scenario, such as negotiating a multimillion-dollar enterprise software deal, where AI-driven clients push back with unexpected objections and concerns.

While these applications exist in early forms today, the future of AI-enhanced VR/AR sales training could become even more advanced. For example, companies can take their VR/AR training to the next level by integrating the following:

- **Real-time emotional and behavioral feedback:** AI analyzes facial expressions, body language, and speech patterns to provide instant feedback. If a salesperson appears too aggressive or uncertain, the system could coach them on refining their approach.

- **Real-world data simulation:** Imagine an AR tool that overlays customer data during sales meetings—displaying past purchases, pain points, and competitor usage directly in the rep's field of vision. This allows real-time pitch adaptation, emphasizing cost savings when budget concerns appear or highlighting integration features when competitor data surfaces, ensuring the most relevant message delivery without extensive preparation.

- **Multiplayer VR sales training:** Sales teams from around the world could meet in a virtual environment where they practice handling client objections, delivering presentations, and refining sales strategies collaboratively, like how multiplayer gaming works today.

By integrating AI-driven VR/AR simulations, sales professionals can experience realistic, high-stakes role-playing that feels as authentic as real-world interactions. Whether it's perfecting a pitch, handling objections under pressure, or refining body language, these technologies will allow for deeper learning, real-time coaching, and a more immersive, data-driven approach to sales training.

While some of the applications previously mentioned are already in play, the next decade will likely bring even more interactive, intelligent, and emotionally aware virtual sales environments—transforming how professionals practice, learn, and master the art of selling.

The Confidence Catalyst

What makes AI role-playing truly transformative is the way repeated success in realistic simulations builds genuine, lasting confidence. This isn't about false bravado; it's about earned expertise through deliberate practice.

The best way to build lasting confidence is through what I call a "Mastery Marathon." This marathon is a series of increasingly challenging scenarios spread over a few months. Here's a sample progression:

Month 1: Foundation Building

- Morning: Basic property presentations
- Afternoon: Record and review sessions
- AI focus: Core communication skills

Month 2: Technical Mastery

- Morning: Feature explanation drills
- Afternoon: Market analysis practice
- AI focus: Accuracy and confidence

Month 3: Objection Handling

- Morning: Common objection scenarios

- Afternoon: Complex negotiation practice

- AI focus: Adaptability and resilience

Month 4: Advanced Integration

- Morning: Multiparty negotiations

- Afternoon: Crisis scenario handling

- AI focus: Comprehensive skill integration

6

AI in the Driver's Seat: Turning Data into Smarter Sales Moves

In today's sales landscape, data-driven decision-making isn't just a competitive advantage—it's a survival skill. The days of relying solely on gut instinct and cold calls are fading fast. Instead, sales teams must leverage real-time insights, predictive analytics, and AI-powered automation to close deals efficiently and outperform competitors.

Sarah was about to find that out, as she stood in her conference room, looking at her laptop screen projected onto the large wall monitor. Her CRM dashboard displayed market trend data, client feedback patterns, and performance metrics that updated throughout the day as new information came in. Her team had grown significantly, they were improving their customer service through role-playing, and her various business intelligence tools were generating more insights than ever before. But she was grappling with analysis paralysis—the challenge of turning an abundance of data into actionable decisions.

Three hundred miles away, Michael faced his own version of this challenge. His loan officers were receiving real-time AI guidance during client conversations, but he noticed an interesting pattern: Some loan officers were flowing naturally with the AI's suggestions, while others seemed to freeze up, caught between their instincts and the system's recommendations.

"It was like having a GPS that could predict traffic patterns, weather changes, and road conditions," Michael explained, "but some drivers were still missing exits because they were too focused on the navigation screen instead of the road."

AI should be treated as a copilot for sales professionals, helping with everything from lead prioritization and customer sentiment analysis to real-time objection handling and sales forecasting. It enables businesses to process vast amounts of data quickly, spot patterns that humans might miss, and make informed, strategic decisions at scale.

The integration of artificial intelligence into sales processes marks a transformative shift in how organizations approach decision-making and customer engagement. As we venture deeper into the digital age, the marriage of AI and sales expertise has created unprecedented opportunities for organizations to enhance their decision-making capabilities, optimize customer interactions, and drive superior business outcomes.

This chapter presents a comprehensive framework for understanding and implementing AI-powered sales strategies, supported by real-world applications and practical implementation guidelines.

To understand how AI fits into sales decision-making, we must examine a three-pillar framework that forms the foundation of successful AI integration in sales. Each pillar builds upon the previous one, creating a robust foundation for AI-driven sales excellence.

PILLAR 1. DATA COLLECTION AND PREPARATION: FEEDING THE AI BEAST

The journey toward AI-powered sales excellence begins with data. Before AI can provide meaningful insights, it requires structured, relevant data. The old axiom "garbage in, garbage out" holds particularly true in the context of AI-driven sales decisions—no amount of sophisticated AI can compensate for poor quality data.

Modern sales teams are increasingly integrating AI with their CRM systems, whether they use Salesforce, HubSpot, or Pipedrive. These integrations enable comprehensive tracking of every customer interaction, from initial website visits to final purchases. The AI systems then process this raw data, cleaning and structuring it for accurate analysis.

Several powerful tools have emerged to support this crucial data preparation phase. OpenAI's GPT-5 has proven particularly valuable for summarizing and cleaning datasets, especially when dealing with unstructured data like customer feedback or sales notes. Traditional data science tools like Pandas and NumPy remain essential for structuring sales data, while specialized platforms like Alteryx and Talend excel at data wrangling and preparation.

PILLAR 2. DATA ANALYSIS AND PATTERN RECOGNITION: THE AI SUPERPOWER

Once clean, structured data is available, AI systems begin their real work: identifying trends, correlations, and anomalies that can optimize sales strategies. This capability represents AI's true superpower in the sales context, as it can process and analyze volumes of data far beyond human capacity.

Consider a real-world example. Through AI analysis, one sales team discovered that their enterprise leads from LinkedIn had a 35 percent higher conversion rate compared to cold emails. This insight, which might have taken months to discover through conventional analysis, was revealed through AI pattern recognition in a matter of days. Similarly, AI analysis uncovered that deals often stalled after the second follow-up email, suggesting the need for a revised engagement strategy.[1]

ChatGPT has emerged as a powerful tool for summarizing patterns in sales data, with prompts like "Analyze this sales dataset and identify key purchasing trends." IBM watsonx AI provides deep-dive business intelligence capabilities, while Tableau has integrated AI-powered features that transform raw sales data into actionable visualizations, making complex patterns accessible to sales teams of all technical levels.

PILLAR 3. REAL-TIME AI GUIDANCE: YOUR VIRTUAL SALES COACH

The third pillar of our framework moves beyond historical analysis to active, real-time assistance. This is where AI transforms from an analytical tool into a virtual sales coach, providing immediate guidance during customer interactions.

Tools like Gong.io and Chorus.ai have revolutionized sales calls by providing real-time objection handling while analyzing ongoing conversations. Email optimization platforms like Drift Email have introduced AI capabilities that personalize messages and adjust tone based on customer sentiment analysis. Perhaps most impressively, AI systems now offer real-time pricing recommendations by analyzing competitor offers and detecting prospect urgency signals.

The technology stack for real-time guidance has also expanded significantly in the recent months. H2O.ai has established itself as a leader in

AI-powered sales predictions, while Amazon SageMaker enables sophisticated real-time sales automation and pricing models. Google AI's Vertex AI has emerged as a powerful platform for enterprise-level decision-making automation.

REAL-WORLD CASE STUDY
ACI Corporation's AI-Powered Sales Coaching

ACI Corporation, a health insurance company, implemented Salesken's real-time sales agent assistance to address low conversion rates and inefficient lead qualification. The AI system provided real-time prompts and guidance during calls. The results were impressive:

- **Sales conversions increased from under 5** percent **to 6.5** percent. Before integrating Salesken, ACI's sales conversion rate struggled to surpass 5 percent, meaning that a large portion of potential customers were not progressing through the sales funnel. With real-time, AI-driven coaching, agents received instant prompts on how to handle objections, personalize their pitch, and emphasize key value propositions based on customer responses. These strategic enhancements boosted conversion rates to 6.5 percent, leading to a measurable increase in revenue.

- **Qualified leads increased from 45.5** percent **to 64.1** percent. One of the most significant challenges for ACI's sales team was identifying high-quality leads efficiently. Prior to AI integration, nearly 55 percent of potential leads were either irrelevant or unqualified, leading to wasted resources and reduced efficiency. By leveraging AI-driven insights, agents could better assess customer intent, needs, and budget suitability in real time, allowing them to focus on high-potential prospects. As a result, the percentage of qualified leads jumped from 45.5 percent to 64.1 percent, drastically improving the sales pipeline.

continued

- **Product knowledge among sales agents increased from 24** percent **to 34.6** percent. ACI Corporation also struggled with sales agents lacking in-depth knowledge of the company's diverse health insurance products. Salesken's AI provided real-time educational nudges during conversations, ensuring that agents communicated the right features and benefits to customers based on their unique requirements. Over time, this proactive knowledge reinforcement improved the agents' product expertise from 24 percent to 34.6 percent, leading to more confident and effective sales interactions.[2]

THE RISE OF CONVERSATION INTELLIGENCE PLATFORMS

An AI that analyzes sales calls or presentations is typically referred to as a "conversation intelligence" platform. These platforms use machine learning to transcribe and analyze recorded sales interactions, providing insights into customer sentiment, key talking points, and overall call effectiveness. These platforms also provide insights on talk time, active listening, and objection handling, which allows for coaching and performance improvement within sales teams. Popular examples include Gong.io, Chorus.ai, Dialpad, and Salesloft.

Let's examine specific AI configurations that organizations have used successfully.

REAL-TIME ANALYSIS CONFIGURATION

A global retail chain can implement this framework for their store managers:

AI Decision Support Setup:

Role: Real-time business analyst

Primary focus: Sales and inventory optimization

Input analysis:

- Real-time sales data
- Customer traffic patterns
- Inventory levels
- Staff availability
- Historical performance data

Output requirements:

1. Immediate insights
   a. Clear action recommendations
   b. Confidence level indicators
   c. Supporting data summary
2. Trend detection
   a. Pattern identification
   b. Anomaly alerts
   c. Opportunity flags
3. Response format:
   a. Priority level (high/medium/low)
   b. Recommended action
   c. Supporting data (three key points max)
   d. Alternative options (if confidence <90 percent)

CUSTOMER INTERACTION SUPPORT

Here's how a telecommunications company can configure their AI support for customer service representatives:

Real-time guidance system:

Role: Customer experience optimizer

Context: Live customer interactions

Monitoring parameters:

- Customer sentiment analysis
- Historical interaction patterns
- Product usage data
- Recent service issues
- Solution effectiveness rates

Guidance protocol:

1. Listen for key triggers.
2. Analyze context in real time.
3. Provide suggested responses.
4. Monitor outcome.
5. Adjust approach based on results.

Alert conditions:

- Negative sentiment detection
- Escalation risk
- Opportunity for upsell
- Service recovery needed

MARKET ANALYSIS AND DECISION SUPPORT

A real estate team can use this configuration for market trend analysis:

Market intelligence system:

Objective: Real-time market insights

Scope: Property valuation and client guidance

Data integration:

- Market trends
- Comparable sales

- Economic indicators
- Buyer behavior patterns
- Local development plans

Analysis requirements:

1. Price trend detection
   a. 30-/60-/90-day patterns
   b. Seasonal adjustments
   c. Market segment analysis
2. Buyer behavior analysis
   a. Search pattern changes
   b. Preference shifts
   c. Demographic trends
3. Opportunity identification
   a. Market gaps
   b. Timing recommendations
   c. Risk assessments

PROCESS OPTIMIZATION FRAMEWORK

A manufacturing company can implement this system for their production line managers:

Operational excellence monitor:

Focus: Production optimization

Time frame: Real-time and predictive

Monitoring elements:

- Equipment performance
- Quality metrics
- Resource utilization
- Staff productivity
- Supply chain status

> Decision support protocol:
> 1. Current state analysis
>   a. Performance vs. targets
>   b. Resource allocation
>   c. Quality indicators
> 2. Predictive insights
>   a. Maintenance needs
>   b. Resource requirements
>   c. Quality trend analysis
> 3. Action recommendations
>   a. Priority ranking
>   b. Resource impact
>   c. Expected outcomes

ADVANCED AI-POWERED SALES STRATEGIES: REAL-WORLD IMPACT

The real-world impact of AI on sales decision-making is best illustrated through concrete examples. Look at Netflix's approach to content recommendation. Netflix's AI analyzes millions of viewing habits to recommend personalized content to its customers.[3] Sales teams can take a similar approach by analyzing prospect engagement data to predict which leads are most likely to convert, allowing representatives to focus their efforts on high-value opportunities.

Walmart's implementation of AI for inventory and demand forecasting offers another instructive example. Walmart uses AI to analyze historical sales data, online searches, weather patterns, macroeconomic trends, and local demographics to optimize product placement, predict demand, and adjust inventory flows across both physical and digital channels.[4] Sales professionals can apply similar principles using AI-driven forecasting tools like Clari or Aviso to anticipate seasonal demand spikes and adjust their outreach strategies accordingly.

Sephora's success with AI-powered recommendations demonstrates the power of personalization in driving conversions. Their AI system looks at user behaviors—such as search queries, browsing history, click-through rates, purchase history, and quiz results—and recommends products that align with the customer's expressed preferences, current context, and even sentiment from reviews. This has boosted Sephora's in-store conversions by 18 percent, a result that sales teams can emulate by using AI to personalize product recommendations based on prospect interaction history.[5]

Leading platforms like HubSpot Sales Hub and Salesforce Einstein have integrated sophisticated AI-powered lead scoring capabilities. Hubspot's AI analyzes data from website behavior, email engagement, and CRM interactions to score and prioritize leads, ensuring sales teams focus on the prospects most likely to convert. Salesforce Einstein uses machine learning to predict which leads are most likely to convert by evaluating demographic, engagement, and historical data.[6]

These systems can be enhanced further through strategic use of GPT models, which can analyze lead lists and prioritize prospects based on likelihood to convert using historical engagement data as a guide. For example, sales teams can leverage GPT models with specific prompts like "Analyze this lead list and prioritize the top ten based on likelihood to convert, using past engagement data." This prompt, when combined with your lead data, helps focus sales efforts on the most promising opportunities.

Sales coaching and performance optimization have been transformed by AI-powered tools that analyze successful sales calls and provide real-time feedback. Platforms like Gong.io track top performers and suggest best practices, while Mindtickle offers AI-driven sales training that adapts to individual learning patterns.

Sales professionals can accelerate their improvement by using prompts such as: "Analyze my last three sales calls and provide feedback on what I can improve." This type of prompt helps identify specific areas for enhancement while providing actionable recommendations based on successful patterns.

Competitive analysis has also evolved with AI integration. Modern sales teams leverage AI tools like Crayon and Kompyte to maintain up-to-date battlecards and competitive intelligence. These systems can automatically track competitor updates and suggest optimal positioning strategies.

To maintain a competitive edge, sales teams can utilize prompts such as: "Summarize the key differentiators between our software and [competitor] based on their latest updates." This approach ensures that sales teams always have access to the most current competitive intelligence and can position their offerings effectively.

EXTRACTING INSIGHTS WITH CHATGPT DATA ANALYSIS

I have mentioned how AI can help you analyze data, find patterns, and detect anomalies. So before I wrap up this chapter, I want to give you a step-by-step guide on how to analyze data and extract insights using ChatGPT data analysis.

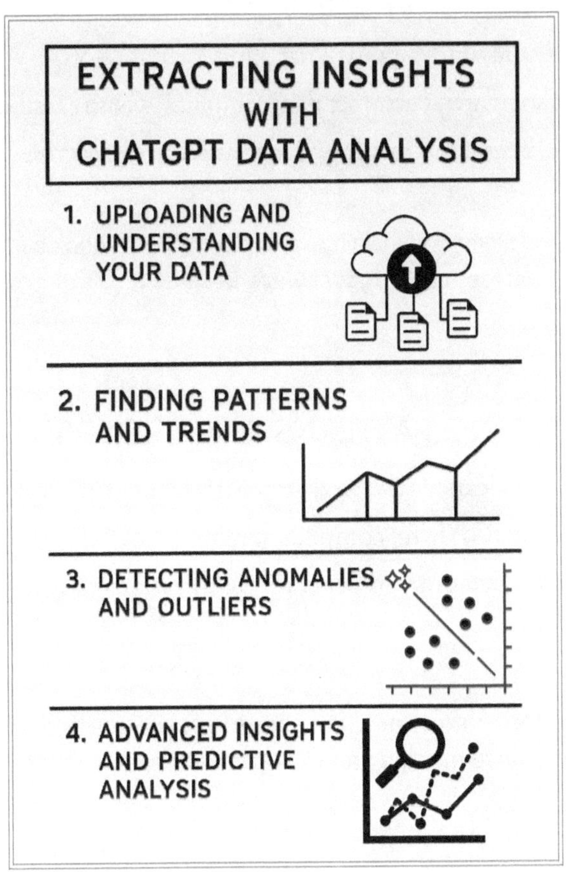

STEP 1: UPLOADING AND UNDERSTANDING YOUR DATA

The first step in using ChatGPT's data analysis capabilities is to upload your dataset (typically in CSV, Excel, or JSON format) and let the AI analyze its structure. You can start by asking ChatGPT:

Can you summarize the contents of this dataset and highlight the key variables?

This helps you understand what kind of data you're working with, whether it's sales figures, customer demographics, website traffic, or financial records. If the dataset has missing or inconsistent values, you can prompt:

> Identify any missing values or inconsistencies in this dataset and suggest ways to clean it.

STEP 2: FINDING PATTERNS AND TRENDS

Once the data is cleaned, the next step is to identify patterns and trends. You can ask ChatGPT to compute summary statistics (mean, median, mode, standard deviation) or generate visualizations to reveal trends. For instance:

> Generate a line chart showing sales growth over the past twelve months and highlight any seasonal patterns.

If you're working with customer data, you might ask:

> Analyze purchase history to find the most common buying trends among different age groups.

By using correlation analysis, you can also determine how variables are related. For example, a real estate analyst might prompt:

> Find correlations between home prices and factors like square footage, location, and number of bedrooms.

STEP 3: DETECTING ANOMALIES AND OUTLIERS

One of the most valuable aspects of data analysis is identifying outliers and anomalies, which can signal fraud, errors, or unique insights. You can prompt:

> Detect any unusual spikes or drops in website traffic over the past year and suggest possible reasons.

For financial data, you might ask:

> Find any transactions that significantly deviate from the average pattern and could indicate fraud.

Using statistical techniques like z-scores or box plots, ChatGPT can highlight data points that fall far outside the normal range.

STEP 4: ADVANCED INSIGHTS AND PREDICTIVE ANALYSIS

Once you've identified trends and anomalies, you can move on to predictive analysis, where AI can help forecast future outcomes based on historical data. For example:

> Based on past sales trends, predict the revenue for the next quarter.

If working with customer churn, you might ask:

> Identify patterns among customers who canceled their subscriptions and predict which current users are at risk of churning.

ChatGPT can also assist with clustering and segmentation, such as grouping customers based on behavior to tailor marketing strategies.

By following these steps—understanding your data, finding patterns, detecting anomalies, and making predictions—you can extract meaningful insights and drive smarter decision-making using AI-powered analysis.

REAL-WORLD CASE STUDY: FROM FORECASTING CHAOS TO 95 PERCENT ACCURACY

How Upwork Transformed Revenue Predictability

When Upwork's revenue operations team pushed aggressively into enterprise sales, they hit a wall. Their forecasting methodology—built on historical data and spreadsheet models—couldn't keep pace with organizational change. Drew Korab, director of Revenue Operations, faced a problem familiar to scaling companies: forecast accuracy swinging wildly by double digits each quarter.

The Breaking Point

The legacy process was incredibly inefficient. Multiple teams maintained separate spreadsheets, pulling data manually from Salesforce. Sales representatives submitted projections based largely on gut feelings. The entire apparatus consumed six hours weekly across five meetings, with managers spending additional hours chasing down missing submissions. On average weeks, only 75 percent of reps submitted forecasts on time.

For a publicly traded company navigating economic uncertainty while launching new go-to-market strategies, this unreliability was impossible to sustain. Quarter-over-quarter comparisons lost predictive value when the business itself was changing. Leadership couldn't confidently guide the board or investors with unreliable data.

The Transformation

Upwork reimagined their approach by anchoring forecasts in objective conversation data rather than manual CRM updates. Instead of relying on representatives to remember updating opportunity stages—updates that happen sporadically and carry inherent optimism bias—the team now accessed real-time deal health signals from actual customer interactions.

They established a streamlined weekly rhythm: daily pipeline inspections with automated risk alerts, midweek forecast submissions with automated reminders, Thursday reviews using AI-powered deal assessments, and Friday top-down validation. This structure cut forecasting time in half while achieving 100 percent on-time submission rates.

The Impact

Within three quarters, Upwork achieved 95 percent forecast accuracy—remarkable for any organization, especially one undergoing strategic transformation. This precision delivered benefits throughout the company. C-suite executives gained confidence in numbers driving strategic decisions, and the improved capability provided stability during economic turbulence. As Mike Schaffer, vice president of Revenue Operations noted, while no one can predict how uncertainties will resolve, reliable internal data positions organizations to respond effectively regardless of external circumstances. Additionally, daily visibility into pipeline health fundamentally changed decision-making. Rather than waiting for quarterly results, teams receive continuous feedback on initiatives, enabling rapid strategy adjustments.

This case illustrates a broader trend: organizations are shifting from periodic backward-looking analysis toward continuous forward-looking intelligence.[7]

SIX SALES STRATEGIES FOR BUILDING A POWERFUL AI-DRIVEN APPROACH

Developing a sales strategy powered by AI isn't as simple as flipping a switch and watching the revenue roll in. Like any great innovation, it requires careful planning, thoughtful execution, and occasionally, a reality check when your chatbot starts recommending cat food to a B2B executive. To harness AI's full potential and drive substantial growth, consider these six foundational strategies.

1. PUT CUSTOMER EXPERIENCE FIRST— NOT JUST DATA POINTS

If AI were a salesperson, it would be the one who remembers your favorite coffee order but also suggests a yacht when you are browsing for a bicycle. The key is using AI to enhance, not replace, human connection. By analyzing customer behavior, identifying common pain points, and tailoring solutions, AI can personalize sales interactions at scale. According to Salesforce, 73 percent of customers expect companies to understand their needs and deliver relevant experiences.[8] By leveraging AI to provide proactive recommendations and instant support, businesses can boost satisfaction, build trust, and ultimately drive conversions.

2. LET DATA BE YOUR COMPASS, NOT A CRYSTAL BALL

AI thrives on data—give it plenty to chew on, and it will reveal insights that even your most seasoned sales reps might miss. Use AI-driven analytics to assess customer preferences, identify purchasing patterns, and refine your targeting. A study by McKinsey found that data-driven sales organizations are twenty-three times more likely to outperform competitors in acquiring new customers.[9] Instead of relying on intuition (or last quarter's best guess), allow AI to predict which leads are worth pursuing and when, because even the best sales pitch won't work if it lands at the wrong time.

3. WALK BEFORE YOU RUN: IMPLEMENT AI IN PHASES

Rolling out AI across your entire sales process in one go is like jumping into a self-driving car without checking if the brakes work: Gradual integration is key. Start with smaller implementations, such as AI-powered lead scoring, automated email follow-ups, or chatbots for initial inquiries. As your team becomes comfortable, expand AI's role into more complex functions like predictive analytics and automated negotiation tools. Companies that adopt AI incrementally see higher adoption rates and fewer operational disruptions compared to those that dive in headfirst.

4. TRAIN YOUR SALES TEAM (SO THEY DON'T FEAR THE AI TAKEOVER)

Your team's first reaction to AI might range from excitement to existential dread ("Will this thing take my job?"). Education is crucial. AI isn't here to replace human salespeople—it's here to supercharge their efforts. Offer hands-on training sessions to demonstrate how AI tools can help close deals faster, automate tedious tasks, and provide data-backed insights that make prospecting easier. Encourage a culture of continuous learning, as AI is evolving rapidly. Today's cutting-edge tool might be yesterday's news in a year.

5. KEEP SCORE: MONITOR, MEASURE, AND MODIFY

If you're not tracking AI's performance, you're essentially throwing darts in the dark and hoping one lands on the bullseye. Define clear key performance indicators such as lead conversion rates, customer retention, and sales cycle speed. AI tools can provide real-time dashboards that highlight what's working and what needs fine-tuning. Regular reviews ensure that your AI strategy is delivering actual value—not just flashy automation with no real impact. A/B testing different AI-driven approaches (such as messaging styles or pricing algorithms) can further refine results over time.

6. PARTNER WITH AI EXPERTS—BECAUSE EVEN AI NEEDS A HUMAN TOUCH

Even the best AI tools require expert guidance to ensure seamless integration and peak performance. Partnering with AI consultants or tech firms can help you select the right tools, troubleshoot challenges, and design a scalable AI road map. Boston Consulting Group's "Where's the Value in AI?" report shows that companies using AI for personalized marketing and related functions can see approximately 30 percent productivity gains in those areas.[10] Think of it as hiring an AI coach—because even the smartest algorithm needs a human quarterback to call the plays.

As "the AI Coach" for several businesses, this is exactly what I specialize in, and I can testify that the companies I work with see not just faster adoption but significant improvement in efficiency, productivity, and skill level.

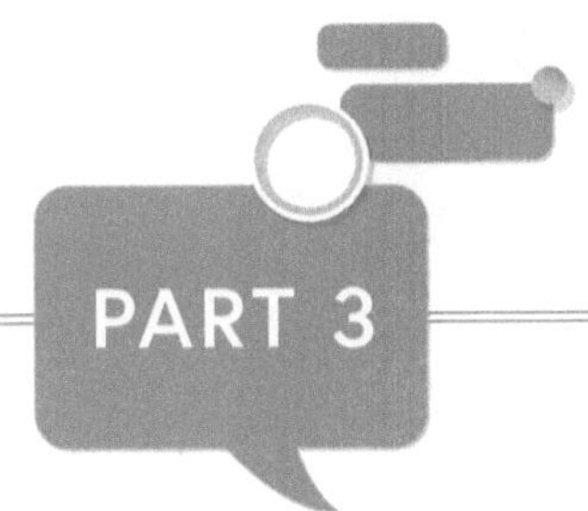

COACHING IN MARKETING:

AI'S ROLE IN CREATIVE STRATEGY AND CAMPAIGN SUCCESS

7

Marketing's New Muse: AI-Powered Creativity and Strategy

In the last section, we explored how AI, when positioned as a coach, can revolutionize the sales process by reinforcing effective behaviors, delivering real-time feedback, and accelerating growth. Now, we turn our attention to the marketing function—an area where creativity, strategy, and data must work in harmony.

After Sarah and her team successfully implemented AI for role-playing training and trend analysis, she began to see patterns emerging across her business operations. The AI coaching system had not only improved her agents' performance but had also generated valuable insights about client preferences and market behaviors. This success sparked a realization: If AI could transform her training and analytics, why not apply it to her marketing efforts as well?

Sarah recognized that her team's marketing strategies—from social media posts to email campaigns—could benefit from the same data-driven approach that had revolutionized their sales process. She wanted to examine how her team currently reached potential clients and explore whether AI could help them create more targeted, effective marketing campaigns that would generate higher-quality leads for her newly trained sales force.

THE CONTENT CREATION REVOLUTION

Sarah's journey began with using AI to understand exactly what content her audience needed. Here's how she started:

Audience analysis prompt:

Role: Marketing strategy analyst

Task: Analyze my target real estate market audience.

Input parameters:

Geographic location: [Local market details]

- Recent property sales data
- Social media engagement metrics
- Website analytics
- Customer feedback and queries

Output requirements:

1. Identify primary audience segments
2. Content preferences by segment
3. Key pain points and interests
4. Optimal content types and channels
5. Engagement patterns and timing

The AI's analysis revealed patterns she hadn't noticed. For example, they discovered that their luxury property buyers were most engaged with video content early in the week, while first-time homebuyers preferred detailed written guides posted on the weekends. This discovery completely changed their content strategy.

FROM ANALYSIS TO ACTION: THE CONTENT CALENDAR

Sarah realized that they needed to create a content calendar that was strategic and addressed the issues the AI's analysis found. A content calendar is essentially a master schedule that maps out what marketing content will be published, when, and across which channels—think of it as a road map that ensures your messaging stays consistent, timely, and aligned with your business goals. Rather than posting randomly or scrambling for content ideas at the last minute, a well-structured content calendar helps businesses maintain regular engagement with their audience while strategically addressing different stages of the customer journey.

Sarah created her team's strategic content calendar with this prompt:

Content calendar creation:

Goal: Three-month content strategy for real estate agency

Requirements:

- Mix of content types (video, text, social, email)
- Platform-specific content
- Audience segment targeting
- Key themes and topics
- Posting schedule with optimal timing
- Content repurposing opportunities

Special focus:

- Seasonal trends

- Market conditions
- Local events
- Property type mix

The AI generated a comprehensive content calendar that included:

- Weekly market update videos

- Biweekly neighborhood spotlight blogs

- Daily social media posts across platforms

- Monthly email newsletters

- Property showcase presentations

- Educational content for first-time buyers

CREATING COMPELLING PROPERTY DESCRIPTIONS

Sarah's challenge became clear when she realized her team was spending hours each week writing property descriptions that often sounded remarkably similar. Generic phrases like "charming home" and "great location" appeared in nearly every listing, making it difficult for potential buyers to distinguish between properties or understand what made each one special.

With her newly implemented content calendar calling for fresh social media posts, email campaigns, and website updates featuring different properties each week, Sarah needed a way to generate compelling, unique descriptions at scale. The challenge wasn't just volume—it was creating content that would capture the distinct personality of each property while appealing to the right target audience, whether that was young families, luxury buyers, or investment-minded clients.

Her testing ground was creating unique descriptions for twenty different properties. Here's how she approached it:

Property description framework:

Property type: [Specific details]

Target audience: [Buyer persona]

Unique features: [List key attributes]

Neighborhood details: [Area information]

Style requirements:

- Emotional connection
- Unique value proposition
- Storytelling elements
- Search engine optimization (SEO)
- Call to action

For a historic downtown loft, the AI helped craft this narrative:

Where industrial heritage meets modern luxury, this transformed 1920s textile mill tells a story of urban renaissance. Soaring fourteen-foot ceilings and original brick walls frame contemporary living spaces, while energy-efficient updates ensure modern comfort. Steps from the arts district, this home isn't just a residence—it's a piece of city history reimagined for today's urban adventurer.

SOCIAL MEDIA MASTERY

Sarah's next challenge was creating engaging social media content across multiple platforms. Each platform needs its own voice, but maintaining consistency across all of them can be a nightmare. Here's how she used AI to solve this:

Platform-specific content generator:

Platform: [Instagram/Facebook/LinkedIn/Twitter(X)]

Property type: [Specific details]

Core message: [Key selling points]

Brand voice: [Style guidelines]

Content requirements:

- Platform-appropriate format
- Relevant hashtags
- Engagement hooks
- Call to action
- Image description suggestions

For a luxury beachfront property, this generated platform-specific posts.

Instagram

Experience sunset dreams

Swipe to discover five unique features that make this ocean-front masterpiece the ultimate coastal retreat. #LuxuryLiving #CoastalHome #DreamHouse

LinkedIn

Investment opportunity alert: Just listed—premium beachfront property

- 5,200 sq. ft. of innovative design
- 10 percent above-market rental potential
- Emerging luxury neighborhood
- Smart-home integration. Contact us for detailed investment analysis and market projections.

X (Twitter) Thread:

1/5—Just Listed

Where luxury meets the ocean

A thread about why this property is making waves in the [area] market . . .

2/5—The Numbers That Matter

- 5,200 sq. ft. of living space
- 180-degree ocean views
- 4-car garage
- Private beach access

3/5—Smart Living, Elevated

Why choose between luxury and convenience when you can have both?

This home is equipped with state-of-the-art smart-home tech, allowing you to control lighting, climate, and security—right from your phone!

Would you upgrade to a fully connected home? Let us know!

#SmartHome #LuxuryLiving #ModernComfort

. . . Followed by 4/5 and 5/5

Next, video content was also crucial for engagement. Here's how Sarah approached video script creation.

Video script generator:

Type: Property showcase

Duration: Ninety seconds

Style: Modern, engaging, professional

Elements to include:

- Attention-grabbing opener
- Key property highlights
- Unique selling points
- Neighborhood features
- Call to action

Technical requirements:

- Shot suggestions
- B-roll recommendations
- Music mood
- Pacing notes

Sample Video Script Output

Here's a detailed property showcase video script that aligns with your requirements.

- **Duration:** Ninety seconds
- **Style:** Modern, engaging, professional
- **Music:** Upbeat, sophisticated background music with a subtle build-up

[Opening scene: Aerial drone shot over the property]

Narrator (energetic, engaging tone):

"Welcome to your dream home! Nestled in the heart of [neighborhood name], this stunning [property type] is more than just a house—it's a lifestyle upgrade waiting for you!"

[Cut to: Slow-motion shot of the home's exterior—luxurious entrance, pristine landscaping]

"With [X] bedrooms, [X] bathrooms, and [square footage] of elegant living space, this home offers both comfort and sophistication."

Key Property Highlights

[Cut to living room: Wide shot, slow push-in]

"Step inside and be greeted by an open-concept design, soaring ceilings, and an abundance of natural light. Perfect for entertaining or cozy family nights in."

[Cut to kitchen: Top-down and close-up shots of marble countertops and high-end appliances]

"The gourmet kitchen features top-of-the-line [brand] appliances, custom cabinetry, and a spacious island—ideal for culinary enthusiasts."

[Cut to master bedroom: Slow pan across luxurious bed and large windows with a scenic view]

"Your private sanctuary awaits. The master suite is a retreat of its own, complete with a spa-like en suite and a walk-in closet designed for style and function."

[Cut to bathroom: Water running over sleek countertops and steam rising from the shower]

"Every detail has been designed for relaxation, from the rainfall shower to the deep soaking tub."

Unique Selling Points

[Cut to backyard: Sunset lighting and firepit or pool area]

"Step outside to your very own oasis. Whether it's summer BBQs, a quiet morning coffee, or a dip in the pool, this space is built for enjoyment."

[Cut to smart-home features: Close-up of a touch-screen panel adjusting lights or thermostat]

"And with smart-home technology, control lighting, temperature, and security—all at your fingertips."

Neighborhood Features

[Cut to local park/trendy café: Top-rated school or nearby beach/ mountain trails]

"Location is everything! [Neighborhood name] offers top-rated schools, vibrant dining, and endless outdoor recreation—all just minutes away."

Call to Action

[Cut to front door shot: Wide shot, inviting perspective]

"This incredible home won't last long! Schedule your private tour today and take the first step toward your dream lifestyle."

[On-screen text: Contact info and call to action; agent's name, phone number, and website]

The output also included shot suggestions, B-roll recommendations, music moods, and pacing notes.

Within a few weeks, Sarah's social media presence had transformed from sporadic, generic posts to a strategic content machine that spoke directly to different client segments across multiple platforms. Her LinkedIn posts were generating meaningful conversations with industry professionals, her Instagram stories were showcasing properties in ways that made followers feel like they were already walking through the front door, and her X updates were positioning her as a go-to market expert.

Most importantly, the time investment had dropped dramatically. What used to take her team hours of brainstorming and writing now happened in minutes, freeing them to focus on client relationships and closing deals. Sarah realized that AI hadn't just improved their marketing; it had given them back the most valuable resource in real estate: time to actually work with people.

PRESENTATION DECK DESIGN

In 2025, Beautiful.ai released an article titled "AI Presentation Design Trends for 2025" that presented how the rapid evolution of AI is reshaping how presentations are designed. Everyone can now make high-quality, engaging visuals, regardless of design expertise. AI-driven presentation tools streamline the process, helping users transform static slides into dynamic, audience-tailored storytelling experiences. The key benefit is efficiency. AI-generated content, smart design suggestions, and real-time adaptability allow professionals to focus on delivering impactful messages without being bogged down by complex design work. As noted by Beautiful.ai's creative director, Danny Chung, on their blog, AI democratizes storytelling, enabling presenters to craft visually compelling narratives that resonate across different generations.[1] One of the biggest trends emerging in AI-driven presentation design is AI-powered, user-generated content that enables users to create professional-grade visuals, text, and layouts with minimal effort. This trend aligns with the growing preference for authenticity and engagement in content marketing. Additionally, AI realism is playing a crucial role by generating highly realistic images, videos, and avatars, which help presenters convey emotions, create relatable testimonials, and enhance storytelling. This ability to bridge the gap between concept and execution is revolutionizing visual communication, making it easier to illustrate ideas in compelling ways.

Another major shift is the rise of AI-powered presentation tools that can analyze and optimize content based on audience feedback and engagement patterns. Modern presentation platforms, such as Beautiful.ai and Gamma.app now offer features like automated design suggestions, content recommendations based on successful templates, and post-presentation analytics that track which slides generated the most engagement. For example, if survey data or feedback forms consistently show that audiences respond better to data-heavy slides versus text-heavy ones, AI can suggest restructuring future presentations to emphasize charts and infographics. Similarly, these tools can analyze successful presentation templates from your organization and recommend similar layouts, color schemes, or content structures that have historically performed well with your target audience. This level of customization increases relevance and engagement, making presentations more effective in diverse professional and educational settings.

The design philosophy in 2025 also shifted toward minimalist maximalism, which blends simplicity with bold, attention-grabbing elements. AI assists in striking this delicate balance by ensuring visual harmony while allowing for creative experimentation. However, as AI-driven design becomes mainstream, concerns around AI hangover—the phenomenon where audiences become fatigued or skeptical of obviously AI-generated content that lacks human authenticity and creativity—are emerging, emphasizing the importance of intentional and meaningful use of AI rather than relying on it as a gimmick. Some designers are also pushing back against AI's ubiquity by embracing an anti-AI aesthetic, favoring more human, organic, and handcrafted design elements to stand out in an increasingly automated landscape.

Ultimately, AI is transforming presentations into immersive, intelligent experiences that cater to the evolving expectations of modern audiences. As tools continue to advance, the focus should remain on using AI to enhance storytelling rather than replacing human creativity. Whether through personalization, real-time adaptability, or bold design choices, AI is poised to redefine how we communicate visually in 2026 and beyond.

For property presentations, Sarah and her real estate team can use AI with Beautiful.ai integration:

Presentation structure:

Type: Luxury property showcase

Platform: Beautiful.ai

Sections required:

1. Property overview
2. Key features
3. Market analysis
4. Investment potential
5. Neighborhood highlights
6. Next steps

Design requirements:

- Clean, minimal aesthetic

- Data visualization preferences
- Image placement suggestions
- Color scheme recommendations

An LLM can provide specific slide-by-slide guidance like the one below, or Beautiful.ai can create actual slides where all you have to do is fill in the blanks and make minor edits and voilà, your slides are ready for an impactful presentation. Here is an example of what the slides can look like:

Luxury Property Showcase: Slide-by-Slide Guide

Slide 1: Property Overview

Goal: Introduce the property with a strong visual impact and key details.

Design and Layout

- Full-width hero image of the property (aerial view or a well-lit facade)
- Minimal text overlay with essential property details
- Property name (or address)
- Bedroom and bathroom count
- Square footage
- Listing price (if applicable)

Color scheme: Elegant tones like deep navy, gold, or crisp white to reflect luxury

Slide 2: Key Features

Goal: Highlight what makes this property unique.

Design and Layout

Two-column format:

- Left side: Text highlights (bullet points for features like high-end finishes, smart-home tech, private pool, custom architecture)

- Right side: High-resolution images (interior shots—living room, kitchen, master suite)
- Use subtle iconography for visual appeal (e.g., a bed icon for bedroom count, a pool icon for outdoor features)

Data visualization:

- Before/after comparison (if the home is newly renovated)
- Infographic-style breakdown of materials used (e.g., "Imported Italian marble countertops")

Slide 3: Market Analysis

Goal: Provide context on property value and market trends.

Design and Layout

- Bar chart or line graph comparing similar properties' pricing in the area
- Pie chart showing market trends (e.g., increase in luxury home values)
- Key data points:
- Recent sales of similar properties
- Market appreciation over the past five years
- Current demand for high-end homes

Color scheme: Neutral with gold or deep blue accents to keep it premium

The next three slides were about investment potential, neighborhood highlights, and finally, call to action (CTA), or next steps.

EMAIL CAMPAIGN SEQUENCES

Email campaigns remain one of the most effective marketing channels, offering direct access to prospects and clients with measurable ROI and personalized messaging capabilities. However, creating compelling email sequences that nurture leads through the entire sales funnel—from initial awareness to final purchase decision—requires strategic planning, consistent messaging, and the ability to segment audiences based on their interests and behaviors.

AI transforms this traditionally time-intensive process by analyzing customer data to suggest optimal send times, personalizing subject lines and content for different audience segments, and automatically adjusting messaging based on engagement patterns. Rather than sending generic blast emails, AI enables marketers to create sophisticated, multi-touch campaigns that feel personally crafted for each recipient while operating at scale.

Let's look at the framework that helped Sarah and her team develop a sophisticated email nurture campaign.

Email sequence generator:

Campaign type: Luxury property launch

Sequence length: Five emails

Target audience: [Specific segment]

Goals:

- Build anticipation.
- Showcase unique features.
- Drive private viewing requests.

Requirements:

- Subject line variations
- Preview text options
- Body content
- CTA progression
- A/B testing suggestions

Here is the actual AI output.

Luxury Property Launch—Five-Email Campaign Sequence

Each email is designed to build anticipation, highlight unique selling points, and drive private viewing requests. Below are subject line variations, preview text options, CTAs, and A/B testing ideas for each stage.

Email 1: The Exclusive Reveal

Goal: Create intrigue and anticipation for the luxury property.

Subject line variations:

- An Exclusive Opportunity Awaits . . .
- A Masterpiece of Luxury—Coming Soon
- You're Invited: A First Look at [Property Name]

Preview text options:

- Be among the first to discover this one-of-a-kind luxury residence.
- A rare opportunity to own a home like no other—details inside.
- The epitome of elegance is about to be unveiled.

CTA progression:

- Soft CTA: *Join the VIP List* (links to an interest form or landing page)
- A/B testing suggestion:
- Test a mystery-driven subject line ("*Something Extraordinary is Coming . . .*") vs. a straightforward luxury appeal ("*Introducing [Property Name]—A New Standard in Luxury*").

Email 2: Unveiling the Masterpiece

Goal: Showcase the most captivating features of the property.

Subject line variations:

- Step Inside a World of Unparalleled Luxury
- The Pinnacle of Design and Elegance—See It Now
- A Home That Redefines Sophistication

Preview text options:

- From breathtaking architecture to world-class amenities—see what sets this home apart.
- An estate where luxury meets innovation. Take a closer look.
- Private spa, infinity pool, panoramic views—this is more than a home; it's an experience.

CTA progression:

- Engagement CTA: *Explore the Gallery* (links to high-end visuals, 3D tour, or video)
- A/B testing suggestion:
  - Test feature-driven subject lines (*"Infinity Pool, Smart Home, Private Spa—It's All Here"*) vs. experience-driven ones (*"A Home That Feels Like a Private Resort"*)

Email 3: The Lifestyle Beyond the Walls

Goal: Highlight location, exclusivity, and lifestyle benefits.

Subject line variations:

- Luxury Living, Perfectly Located
- The Address That Defines Prestige
- A Neighborhood Like No Other

Preview text options:

- Wake up to ocean views, dine at Michelin-starred restaurants, and unwind in your private oasis.
- Surrounded by luxury, convenience, and exclusivity—see what makes this location extraordinary.
- Your home is more than a residence; it's a statement of lifestyle.

CTA progression:

- Interest CTA: *Download the Luxury Brochure* (provides an in-depth digital guide to property and location)

A/B testing suggestion:

- Test a location-driven subject (*"Steps Away from Exclusive Country Clubs & Fine Dining"*) vs. a lifestyle-driven one (*"Live Where Elegance Meets Everyday Convenience"*)

Email 4 was titled: The Invitation—Private Viewings Open, and Email 5 was titled: Final Call—Last Chance for Exclusive Viewings.

BLOG POST DEVELOPMENT

For creating engaging blog content, Sarah used this approach:

Blog Content Framework

Topic: [Specific real estate topic]

Target reader: [Audience segment]

Search engine optimization requirements:
- Primary keyword
- Secondary keywords
- Meta description
- Header structure

Content structure:
- Engaging hook
- Key insights
- Data points
- Expert quotes
- Action steps

Sample Blog Topics Generated

1. Five Hidden Costs of Coastal Property Ownership (and How to Plan for Them)

2. Why Smart Homes Are Redefining Luxury Real Estate in [Area]

3. The Ultimate Guide to Investing in Beachfront Properties

NEWSLETTER STRUCTURING

For monthly market updates, Sarah implemented this system:

Newsletter Template

Type: Monthly market insight

Sections:

1. Market trends overview
2. Featured properties
3. Local development news
4. Expert tips
5. Coming soon preview

Style requirements:

- Data visualization
- Success stories
- Market predictions
- Interactive elements

REAL-WORLD CASE STUDY
Paciolan Boosts Efficiency and Quality with Beautiful.ai

A recent case study from Beautiful.ai highlights how Paciolan's world-class ticketing, marketing, and fundraising platform supports more than 500 live entertainment organizations and processes over 120 million ticket sales each year. To modernize how their teams build and collaborate on presentations, Paciolan turned to Beautiful.ai.

continued

> Formerly a PowerPoint-centric organization, they were looking for a cleaner, more sophisticated way to elevate their slide design and streamline deck creation. With Beautiful.ai, they gained an intuitive, professional tool that upgraded their entire presentation workflow.
>
> Brenda Ramsey, creative director of Paciolan said, "The time savings with Beautiful.ai has been huge. I would say anywhere from 50–75 percent reduction in time. We could have the sales team or other people help with slides, we don't need a designer on hand every minute."[2]

CREATING YOUR DIGITAL DOUBLE: ADVANCED AI CONTENT TOOLS

Another invention that can now make your content creation capabilities take a quantum leap is when you create scalable versions of yourself using AI for video and voice content. Sarah discovered the same and admitted, "At first, it felt a bit sci-fi, but then I realized this was the key to being everywhere without actually being everywhere."

VOICE CLONE CREATION WITH ELEVEN LABS

Artificial intelligence voice technology is reshaping how people create and consume content. Media companies can now quickly produce news stories in multiple languages without hiring different voice actors or spending weeks in production. This technology helps people with visual impairments access written content more easily, and it's ideal for busy listeners who want to absorb information while commuting or exercising. Authors can update their books or create new audio versions without dealing with expensive studio sessions and complicated scheduling, while still maintaining an authentic human sound.

One prominent example of this shift involves Arianna Huffington, who turned to ElevenLabs' voice cloning technology when her best-selling book *Thrive* reached its tenth anniversary. Rather than booking studio time and coordinating schedules, she used an AI replica of her voice to record a new introduction for the audiobook. The approach not only streamlined the entire process but also reduced production costs by thousands of dollars.

Building on this success, the Thrive Global and *The Huffington Post* founder has since incorporated AI voice technology more broadly into her work. Through the Iconic Voices feature in ElevenLabs' Reader app, Huffington now offers her newsletters and articles in audio format using her own cloned voice. Readers can experience her perspectives on wellness and productivity in a more personal, immersive way that goes beyond traditional text.[3]

But it's not just for the rich and famous like Huffington—you, too, can create a replica of your voice that sounds just like you. You can automate video voice-overs, ad reads, podcasts, and more in your voice.

Professional voice cloning capabilities have improved tremendously where the voice clones are now virtually indistinguishable from the real thing. You can clone your voice with only a few minutes of your audio recording.

According to Elevenlabs.io, "We recommend using Professional Voice Cloning to create the perfect voice replica: the minimum here is 30 minutes; three hours is optimal. Instant Voice Cloning (IVC) offers a swift and convenient method to replicate your voice using audio samples as short as one minute, although with comparatively reduced quality. In both cases, results are best if uploaded files comprise clean audio files containing a single speaker with no background noise, music or other effects."[4]

Further, platforms like Eleven Labs support many different languages, which will enable you to create content in languages you don't even speak. You can go from serving one market to reaching international buyers seemingly overnight. The AI handles translation, and you can maintain your brand voice across different languages.

Always inform your audience when using AI-generated voice content (or, for that matter, any AI-generated content). Sarah adds a subtle disclaimer in video descriptions: "Voice-enhanced or generated by AI technology."

YOUR GUIDE TO VIDEO CLONING

If you think cloning your voice sounds like sci-fi, wait till you're able to create a digital twin of yourself.

Enter HeyGen.

After creating your video avatar on HeyGen, there's no need to appear on camera again! Simply write a script, and your avatar will present it just like you would. The creation process takes around five minutes.

First, you will need to record three minutes of video footage. When shooting the footage, use a high-resolution camera, ensure your environment is well lit and quiet, and keep your head centered in the frame. Then upload this footage on HeyGen (after creating your account), and your digital twin will be ready to record on your behalf.[5]

HeyGen, of course, is not the only company that provides this service. Some of the other popular platforms that can create AI-avatar-powered videos are Colossyan, Elai.io, VEED, and Synthesia.

REAL-WORLD CASE STUDY
Trivago's Strategy for
Global Advertising Localization

The travel metasearch giant Trivago discovered an AI solution that cut their ad production timeline in half while expanding their reach across global markets, as presented in a customer story published by HeyGen. What once took three to four months now happens in weeks, allowing the company to deliver localized television commercials in thirty markets with consistent branding and authentic regional appeal. Before adopting HeyGen's platform, Trivago's creative team faced a persistent obstacle in their TV advertising strategy: creating ads that resonated locally across dozens of markets. Trivago's options were limited and flawed. They could hunt for that elusive performer who somehow appealed universally—a search that drained budgets and calendars—or they could overlay different audio tracks onto existing footage, which invariably felt artificial and disconnected. Neither path gave them what they actually needed.

HeyGen's AI technology offered a different route entirely. The platform creates synthetic voices and matching mouth movements in various languages, allowing one on-screen presence to speak authentically to audiences everywhere. When Trivago faced a nonnegotiable launch date, they made the call to trust this relatively new approach. Despite working across different time zones and handling urgent last-minute revisions, the collaboration delivered.

The efficiency gains were substantial. Editing work that used to consume months now wraps up in weeks—specifically, production time dropped by 50 percent. In one three-month sprint, Trivago rolled out customized campaigns across fifteen territories, something their old workflow simply couldn't accommodate. The text-to-speech functionality meant quick regional adjustments without dragging actors back into recording booths.

More importantly, Trivago found a repeatable system. They're not just saving money and time on individual projects—they've established a new operational model for how a global brand can speak to local audiences at scale while keeping its identity intact.[6]

Remember, the journey to AI-enhanced content creation is a marathon, not a sprint. Some days your AI will write pure poetry, and other days it'll try to sell a beachfront property to penguins. The key is learning from both.

Your success with AI content creation won't be measured by how many tools you use but by how effectively you use them to connect with your audience. Start with the prompts in our appendix, adapt them to your needs, and remember that every great content creator—human or AI—started with a single word.

Implementation Blueprint: Your Ninety-Day Launch Plan

The journey to AI-powered content creation requires a systematic approach. Here's how to implement the strategies and tools we've discussed.

PHASE 1: FOUNDATION (DAYS 1–30)

Week 1–2: Setup and Analysis

- Audit existing content
- Define brand voice guidelines
- Set up AI tool accounts (LLM, Beautiful.ai, ElevenLabs, HeyGen)
- Document current metrics as baseline
- Create initial prompt library

Week 3–4: Initial Implementation

- Start with one content type (e.g., property descriptions)
- Test and refine prompts
- Build template library
- Train team on basic tools
- Measure initial results

Pro Tip: "Start small but document everything," Sarah advises. "What worked with one property description often becomes your template for future listings."

PHASE 2: EXPANSION (DAYS 31–60)

Week 5–6: Content Diversification

- Add social media content generation.
- Implement email sequences.
- Begin video content creation.
- Develop presentation templates.
- Start cross-platform posting.

Week 7–8: Advanced Integration

- Launch AI voice generation.
- Create video presenter templates.
- Implement multi-language content.
- Develop automated workflows.
- Begin A/B testing.

PHASE 3: OPTIMIZATION (DAYS 61–90)

Week 9–10: Analytics and Refinement

- Review performance metrics.

- Optimize top-performing content.

- Refine weak performers.

- Update prompt library.

- Enhance automation workflows.

Week 11–12: Scale and Systemize

- Document best practices.

- Create training materials.

- Build scaling frameworks.

- Implement quality controls.

- Plan future expansion.

THE PATH FORWARD

The future of content creation is where AI amplifies human creativity rather than replacing it. Success comes not from trying to automate everything but from finding the right balance between AI efficiency and human insight.

Key Success Principles

- **Start small and think big:** Begin with one content type to establish proficiency before expanding your scope. Master the fundamentals of each format before moving to the next, always keeping sight of long-term strategic goals rather than getting lost in immediate implementation details.

- **Measure everything that matters:** Track performance metrics rigorously to understand what works and what doesn't. Monitor quality consistency across all interactions to ensure standards remain high. Document successful approaches meticulously so they can be replicated and scaled across the organization.

- **Stay human in your approach:** Maintain authentic connections even when using AI tools. Use AI for enhancement, not replacement, ensuring that emotional intelligence remains central to all interactions. The goal is amplification of human capability, not its substitution.

- **Evolve continuously through systematic improvement:** Regular tool evaluation ensures you're using the best available technology for your needs. Ongoing prompt refinement sharpens the precision of AI interactions over time. Constant process improvement creates a culture of innovation where both human skills and AI capabilities advance in tandem.

8

Launch, Learn, Optimize: How AI Makes Your Marketing Smarter

Before we get into campaign optimization, let's first look at how easy it is to create campaigns using GenAI features of large language models (LLMs). The outputs in this chapter are from ChatGPT, but you can experiment with Claude and Gemini, too. Claude seems to do better with long-form content, and Gemini seems to do better for search engine optimization (I guess all Google experience helps).

AD COPY CREATION: THE MULTI-PLATFORM APPROACH

Sarah needed to create compelling ad copy across multiple platforms while maintaining consistency. Here's the prompt that she used for a downtown condo listing:

> For a real estate broker who is promoting an urban down-town condo for first-time homebuyers, can you create ad copies for Facebook, LinkedIn, Instagram, and Google with the following focus: "As an advertising copywriter, create multi-platform ad copy."
>
> Property: Downtown condo with easy accessibility to commute, food, and nightlife
>
> Platforms: Google Ads, Facebook, Instagram
>
> Budget level: First-time homebuyers
>
> Deliverables:
>
> - Google Ads
>   - Three headline variations
>   - Two description variations
>   - Two CTA options
>   - Keywords list
> - Facebook/Instagram
>   - Four primary copy versions
>   - Headline options
>   - Two link descriptions
>   - Hashtag groups
>
> Include character counts and platform-specific formatting.

Here is how the output looks.

**Multi-Platform Ad Copy for Downtown Condo
(First-Time Homebuyers)**

This ad campaign is optimized for Google Ads, Facebook, and Instagram, targeting young professionals and first-time home-buyers seeking an affordable, urban lifestyle with easy access to commuting, dining, and nightlife.

Google Ads Copy

Headline Variations (Max. 30 characters)

- Live in the Heart of Downtown (29)
- Your First Home Awaits! (25)
- Walk to Work, Dine, & Play (27)

Description Variations (Max. 90 characters)

- Modern condo near transit, dining, and nightlife. Own your first home today! (88)
- Affordable downtown living! Easy commute, vibrant nightlife, and move-in ready units! (89)

CTA Options

- Schedule a Tour Today!
- Explore Available Listings!

Keywords List (For Google Ads Optimization)

- Downtown condos for sale
- First-time homebuyer condos
- Affordable condos in [city]
- Urban condos with easy commute
- Condos near public transit
- Buy a condo in downtown

Facebook and Instagram Ad Copy

Primary Copy Variations (Max. 125 characters for mobile ads)

Version 1 (Lifestyle Focused)

"City life, simplified! Own a modern condo with easy access to work, dining, & nightlife. Book a tour today!" (124)

Version 2 (FOMO Driven)

"Why rent when you can own? Affordable downtown condos designed for first-time buyers. DM us for details!" (124)

Version 3 (Community Centric)

"Live where the action is! Walkable downtown condos for sale—
perfect for first-time buyers. Start your journey today!" (122)

Version 4 (Affordability Focused)

"Your dream home in downtown is closer than you think! Own for
less than your rent. Learn more!" (117)

Headline Options (Max. 40 characters)
- Affordable Downtown Living (29)
- Why Rent? Own Your First Home! (33)
- Move-In Ready Urban Condos! (33)

Link Description (Max. 30 characters)
- Schedule a private tour now! (29)
- Explore your future home today! (30)

Hashtag Groups for Instagram
- City living and commute focused
  - #CityLiving #WalkableNeighborhood #DowntownVibes
    #FirstTimeBuyer #LiveWhereYouWork
- Homeownership and lifestyle focused
  - #BuyDontRent #CondoLiving #DreamHome #UrbanLiving
    #FirstHomeJourney

WHY IT WORKS

This campaign blends affordability, lifestyle appeal, and convenience,
ensuring first-time homebuyers see the value of urban condo living. The
ads use clear CTAs, emotional triggers, and platform-optimized messaging
to drive leads and increase engagement.

NOT JUST THE AD CAMPAIGN BUT THE WHOLE NINE YARDS

Let's not forget about our mortgage lender Michael. He's been using AI to train his loan officers, analyze current market trends, and create marketing copies to acquire, convert, and retain more customers. Now he wants to take it one step further. Michael wants to create a weekly content calendar that optimizes the omnichannel strategy, making him look omnipresent: social media, blog posts, email marketing, newsletters, videos—as I said, the whole nine yards. And he wanted AI to not just write content but create a weekly calendar that put all of this together, where his EA had little to do but follow the calendar and copy, paste, and publish the content. Easy-peasy.

Here is the prompt he used:

> As a mortgage lender in Las Vegas, NV, I want to create a weekly content calendar that optimizes the omnichannel strategy, making me look omnipresent via social media posts, blog posts, email marketing, newsletters, videos, and anything else you can think of. The content can be meant for potential buyers but also referral partners like real estate agents, financial planners, and CPAs. Can you create a weekly content calendar that will make me look like an expert in the local market and as a mortgage lender, which will help me get more buyer leads?

Here is what the output looked like:

Here's a structured weekly content calendar designed to position you as a top Las Vegas mortgage expert, enhance your omnichannel presence, and generate buyer leads while engaging real estate agents, financial planners, and CPAs.

Weekly Content Calendar for a Mortgage Lender in Las Vegas

Main Goals

- Establish credibility as a Las Vegas market expert.
- Attract homebuyer leads.
- Engage real estate agents, CPAs, and financial planners.
- Maintain an omnipresent digital footprint.

Monday: Market Update and Financial Insights

- **Social media (post and story):** "Las Vegas Weekly Mortgage Market Update!" (short video or carousel post on interest rates, inventory trends, and home prices)
- **LinkedIn post:** "What This Week's Mortgage Rate Changes Mean for Buyers and Realtors" (tag realtors and financial pros)
- **Instagram reel/TikTok:** "Buy now or wait? Las Vegas market breakdown"
- **Email to referral partners:** "Market Trends Update: What Your Clients Need to Know"
- **YouTube Short/video:** "Las Vegas Home Prices and Mortgage Rates: What's Happening?"
- **Facebook Live/Q&A:** "Ask a Mortgage Pro: What's the Best Loan Option Today?"

Tuesday: Educational and Engagement Day

- **Instagram/Facebook post:** "Mortgage Myths Busted: Can You Really Buy a Home with 3% Down?"
- **Instagram story poll:** "What's your biggest home-buying fear?" (engagement strategy)
- **YouTube Short/TikTok:** "Top 3 Mistakes First-Time Buyers Make in Las Vegas"
- **Blog post:** "How to Get Pre-Approved in Las Vegas: A Step-by-Step Guide"
- **Newsletter segment:** Include the blog post and a "Tip of the Week" for buyers
- **LinkedIn article:** "What CPAs and Financial Planners Need to Know About Today's Mortgage Market"

The LLM goes on to give the calendar for Wednesday, Thursday, Friday, Saturday, and Sunday, and even some bonus monthly content. This strategy ensures that you dominate multiple channels daily while providing high-value content to potential buyers and referral partners.

THE OPTIMIZATION REVOLUTION: BEYOND A/B TESTING

Sarah sat in her weekly marketing review meeting, surrounded by campaign performance data from twenty different property listings, feeling like she was playing the world's most complicated game of "Spot the Difference." Traditional A/B testing had served her and her team well, but in today's fast-moving market, sometimes waiting two weeks to determine a winner wasn't just inefficient—it was potentially costly.

Michael faced a similar challenge with his loan marketing campaigns. By the time he and his team figured out which message was resonating best, the interest rates had changed, making their insights less valuable. They needed the ability to optimize campaigns while they were running.

They were both experiencing what I call the optimization opportunity gap: the growing disparity between how quickly markets change and how long traditional optimization methods take.

Can AI come to rescue?

THE TOOLS OF REAL-TIME OPTIMIZATION

The power of modern campaign optimization comes from combining existing AI tools in smart ways. The key platforms that are making this possible include Google, Facebook, and LinkedIn.

Google Ads Smart Bidding

By combining Google Ads' Smart Bidding with LLM-driven automation, businesses can significantly improve targeting, personalization, and conversion rates. Here's how, in four steps.

1. Target ROAS Bidding: Maximizing Return on Ad Spend with AI

Target return on ad spend (ROAS) bidding in Google Ads is an AI-powered Smart Bidding strategy that automatically adjusts bids to maximize revenue while meeting a specific return goal. Unlike manual bidding, which requires constant monitoring and adjustments, target ROAS leverages machine learning to analyze past conversion data, predict future performance, and optimize bids in real time.

For example, an e-commerce business selling high-end electronics can use target ROAS to ensure that their ad spend is directed toward users most likely to make high-value purchases. By analyzing historical data, Google's algorithm determines which clicks are more valuable and increases bids accordingly.

How LLMs can further enhance performance: Businesses can use LLMs to generate structured prompts that refine their Google Ads strategy. For instance, marketers can input historical sales data and customer behavior patterns into an AI model like ChatGPT to generate insights on ideal bid adjustments. A useful prompt for this scenario would be:

> Analyze my last six months of ad performance data and suggest an optimal target ROAS value based on conversion trends and seasonal demand.

This approach allows businesses to dynamically adjust their ROAS targets without manual intervention, ensuring consistent profitability.

2. Responsive Search Ads: AI-Optimized Ad Copy for Better Performance

Responsive search ads use AI to dynamically mix and match headlines and descriptions to find the best-performing ad variations for different users. This feature allows advertisers to input multiple versions of headlines and descriptions, and Google Ads automatically tests different combinations to optimize for clicks and conversions.

For example, a luxury travel agency promoting high-end vacation packages can provide headlines like "Exclusive Private Island Getaways" and "Luxury Resorts with VIP Service," while also including more generic ones like "Top-Rated Holiday Destinations." Google's AI then determines which combinations work best for different audiences.

How LLMs can enhance this further: Marketers can use LLMs to generate highly targeted ad variations based on audience intent and search behavior. By using an AI-powered tool, businesses can generate optimized headlines and descriptions based on their industry and target demographic. A prompt like "Generate ten compelling search engine optimization (SEO) headlines for a Google responsive search ad promoting eco-friendly luxury hotels in Bali" would provide marketers with a variety of high-converting options, reducing the time spent on A/B testing and manual optimization.

3. Audience Segmentation: AI-Driven Personalization for Higher Conversions

Audience segmentation in Google Ads allows businesses to target specific customer groups based on their online behavior, demographics, and intent. Smart Bidding strategies use machine learning to optimize campaigns for different audience segments, ensuring that the right message reaches the right users at the right time.

For example, a Software as a Service (SaaS) company offering business-to-business (B2B) project management software can create segments for small business owners, enterprise executives, and freelance consultants, each receiving tailored ad creatives and landing pages.

How LLMs can help: Businesses can use LLMs to analyze customer data and predict ideal audience segments based on purchase behavior and engagement history. By inputting customer data into an AI tool, companies can get actionable insights on which segments to prioritize. A useful prompt could be:

> Analyze my Google Ads conversion data and suggest new audience segments with high engagement and conversion potential.

This allows advertisers to discover untapped market segments and craft hyper-personalized campaigns for better ROI.

4. Dynamic Remarketing: Reengaging Users with AI-Powered Ads

Dynamic remarketing takes traditional remarketing a step further by automatically displaying personalized ads featuring products or services users have previously viewed. Google Ads dynamically generates these ads using a product feed, ensuring that past website visitors see relevant promotions based on their browsing history. For example, an online fashion retailer can display carousel ads featuring the exact pair of designer shoes a user added to their cart but didn't purchase. This increases the likelihood of conversion by reinforcing interest with timely, personalized content.

How LLMs can enhance performance: AI can automate remarketing copy generation by analyzing past customer interactions and crafting persuasive messaging. Marketers can use AI-driven tools to tailor ad content based on user engagement levels. A practical prompt could be:

> Generate personalized dynamic remarketing ad copy for users who abandoned their cart on my e-commerce store, emphasizing urgency and limited-time discounts.

This ensures that remarketing messages are compelling, increasing the chances of recovering lost sales with minimal manual effort.

AI-driven insights reduce the guesswork in digital advertising, making campaigns more efficient and profitable while saving marketers valuable time.

Facebook Ads Algorithm

Facebook's sophisticated advertising algorithm represents one of the most powerful tools for businesses seeking to maximize their return on advertising spend. The platform's machine learning system continuously analyzes user behavior, engagement patterns, and conversion data to automatically optimize ad delivery for the best possible results. Unlike traditional advertising where marketers make educated guesses about audience preferences, Facebook's algorithm learns from millions of data points in real time, and it adjusts targeting, bidding, and creative delivery to reach users most likely to take desired actions.

The integration of advanced AI tools like Meta AI and other LLMs has further enhanced the effectiveness of Facebook advertising campaigns. These tools can generate compelling ad copy variations, analyze competitor strategies, and suggest creative elements that resonate with specific audience segments. For example, a real estate agency might use AI to create dozens of property description variations, then let Facebook's algorithm test which versions generate the highest engagement rates. Similarly, e-commerce businesses can leverage AI to generate product descriptions that highlight features most likely to drive conversions based on historical performance data.

The financial impact of these AI-enhanced optimizations can be substantial. Press, a plant-based health food brand, achieved a 40 percent boost in conversions after switching from its standard campaign approach to Meta's Advantage+ shopping campaigns combined with generative AI-powered creative.[1] Similarly, the fintech marketing company Draivi used Meta's video and photo ads to promote loan and credit card applications. A Meta Conversion Lift study showed this approach led to a 39 percent increase in completed registrations, underscoring the impact of AI-driven advertising strategies on measurable business results.[2]

The algorithm's ability to identify micro-audiences, such as users who typically engage with real estate content on weekday evenings or shoppers who browse luxury items but purchase during sales events, allows businesses to reach highly qualified prospects at optimal moments. This precision targeting, powered by AI insights and Facebook's vast user data, transforms advertising from a broad-reach strategy into a highly targeted, ROI-focused investment.

LinkedIn Campaign Manager

Just the way Sarah's team used Facebook Ads' algorithm, Michael's loan team can use LinkedIn's optimization tools for their B2B campaigns. Here's how they can achieve remarkable results combining LLMs with LinkedIn Campaign Manager.

1. Audience Expansion: Reaching the Right Decision-Makers at Scale

Michael's company can target B2B clients—such as real estate brokerages, financial advisors, and commercial property investors—by using LinkedIn's audience expansion feature to scale their reach beyond their initial target list while maintaining relevance.

By leveraging LinkedIn's AI-powered look-alike audiences, mortgage companies can identify professionals with similar job titles, industries, and interests as their best-performing clients. For example, a commercial mortgage lender could target CFOs and financial directors of midsize firms but expand their audience to include high-level controllers and VPs of finance, increasing the pool of potential leads.

How LLMs can enhance performance: LLMs can assist in identifying new potential audience segments by analyzing historical customer data and suggesting similar industries or job roles that might be interested in mortgage solutions. A useful prompt could be:

> Analyze my top-performing LinkedIn ad audiences and suggest additional job roles and industries that could have high engagement with our commercial mortgage solutions.

This allows mortgage companies to expand their audience intelligently without wasting ad spend on low-converting prospects.

2. Bid Management: Maximizing Efficiency with AI-Driven Adjustments

Bid management is crucial for optimizing LinkedIn ad spend, ensuring that mortgage companies maximize visibility without overpaying for impressions or clicks.

By utilizing LinkedIn's automated bidding, lenders can let AI dynamically adjust bids based on engagement likelihood, increasing efficiency.

Michael can run a campaign to generate leads from real estate agencies and can set a target cost per lead while allowing LinkedIn's algorithm to adjust bids in real time for better placements. For example, if a brokerage owner is more likely to engage in the afternoon, the system will increase bids during peak hours and reduce spend when engagement drops.

How LLMs can enhance performance: LLMs can analyze campaign performance data and recommend optimal bid strategies based on past trends. A marketer can use a prompt like:

> Based on the last three months of LinkedIn campaign data, what bidding strategy should we use to lower cost per lead while maintaining conversion rates?

By continuously refining bid strategies with AI insights, mortgage companies can improve ROI and reduce wasteful spending.

3. Creative Rotation: Keeping Ads Fresh and Relevant

Ad fatigue is a common challenge in B2B campaigns, especially when targeting niche audiences such as real estate brokers or investors. LinkedIn's creative rotation feature allows mortgage companies to automatically test different variations of ad creatives—headlines, images, videos, or CTAs—to determine which performs best. A lender promoting its AI-powered loan approval platform might test variations like:

- **Ad A:** "Faster Loan Approvals for Commercial Real Estate—See How!"

- **Ad B:** "Get Mortgage Pre-Approvals 24/7 with AI-Driven Underwriting."

By rotating different creatives, LinkedIn's algorithm will prioritize the highest-performing versions, ensuring continuous engagement.

How LLMs can enhance performance: LLMs can generate multiple high-quality ad variations in seconds, helping marketers test different messaging styles at scale. A marketer could use a prompt like:

> Generate five LinkedIn ad headlines and descriptions that emphasize the speed and efficiency of our commercial mortgage approval process.

This enables a streamlined A/B testing process while keeping messaging fresh and relevant.

4. Engagement Tracking: Optimizing Campaigns Based on Real-Time Insights

Tracking engagement metrics—such as click-through rates (CTR), form submissions, and video watch rates—is essential for refining LinkedIn ad campaigns for mortgage companies.

LinkedIn's conversion tracking and website demographics tools allow businesses to see which job titles, industries, and company sizes are engaging most with their content. For example, if a mortgage lender's ad on investment property loans gets higher engagement from midsize property management firms than independent investors, they can adjust targeting accordingly.

How LLMs can enhance performance: LLMs can analyze engagement data and suggest data-driven optimizations in real time. A marketer can ask:

> Analyze the past month of engagement data from our LinkedIn campaign and suggest which audience segments we should focus on or exclude to improve lead quality.

By leveraging AI-powered insights, mortgage companies can quickly refine their campaigns, ensuring that they invest in high-performing audience segments while reducing spend on low-engagement demographics.

THE CREATIVE OPTIMIZATION FRAMEWORK

Implementing tools like dynamic creative optimization (DCO) allows for the real-time assembly of ad components based on user data, enhancing relevance and engagement. This approach utilizes multivariate testing to determine the most effective combinations of creative elements, optimizing performance across diverse audience segments. Solutions from companies like Clinch and Prescient AI make it easier to implement DCO.

The *Adobe 2025 AI and Digital Trends Report* revealed that 65 percent of senior executives now see AI and predictive analytics as pivotal growth catalysts, particularly through the development of more personalized and impactful creative assets. In addition, 53 percent of those using generative AI report significant gains in team efficiency, and 49 percent note better decision-making via AI-driven insights. The report also highlights that overcoming fragmented data systems and integrating robust privacy frameworks are critical steps toward full-scale adoption and measurable ROI in AI initiatives.[3] As agentic AI emerges, organizations are leveraging autonomous systems to deliver real-time, hyper-personalized experiences that further boost customer engagement and retention.

Regularly tracking engagement metrics such as CTR, conversion rates, and customer acquisition costs is essential. Microsoft's 2024 annual report highlights that integrating AI into its advertising platforms enables marketers to create, manage, and troubleshoot campaigns using natural language and thereby streamlining performance monitoring and iterative optimization. The report specifically notes that Copilot in Microsoft Advertising helps increase campaign ROI by delivering faster asset creation, actionable insights, and troubleshooting via conversational AI. Since Copilot's refresh in late 2024, advertisers have seen campaign CTR increase by up to 1.7 times and customer journeys accelerate by over 30 percent through enhanced AI-powered tools.[4] These advances allow for more responsive adjustment of campaigns based on live performance data, leading to higher efficiency and improved marketing outcomes.

You don't need to have the resources of Microsoft to achieve similar (and dare I say, even better) results. I know a thing or two about beating the giants. When my company InstaMortgage was ranked on the Deloitte Fast Tech 500 list, we were not just the first and only mortgage company to make that list—we ranked higher than household names like Zoom, Pinterest, and Square.

THE CREATIVE CODE: UNLOCKING HIGHER CAMPAIGN PERFORMANCE THROUGH BETTER VISUALS AND COPY

It turns out, creativity isn't just the "fun" part of marketing—it's the performance engine. The difference between a wildly successful campaign and one that fizzles into digital obscurity often comes down to better visuals, sharper copy, and more engaging storytelling. In a world where we have just 1.7 seconds of consumer attention per piece of content, marketers need to ensure that every pixel and every word is working overtime.[5]

So how can you make your creative assets not just good but unforgettable? Here are four ways to supercharge your marketing campaigns through better creative execution.

1. DITCH THE BLAND—MAKE EMOTIONAL STORYTELLING YOUR SUPERPOWER

Humans are hardwired for stories, not sales pitches. Neuroscientists have found that compelling storytelling triggers the release of oxytocin, the hormone that builds trust and emotional connection. In a famous case study, Coca-Cola's "Share a Coke" campaign saw a 7 percent increase in sales simply by replacing its logo with popular names, turning a generic product into a personal and emotional experience.[6] Similarly, Airbnb's "Made Possible by Hosts" campaign used real user stories, resulting in 500 million+ impressions and a 2.5-times higher engagement rate than previous campaigns.[7]

The takeaway? Ditch generic sales copy in favor of stories that make people feel something—joy, nostalgia, FOMO, or even a good old-fashioned tearjerker. When your brand becomes part of their story, you've won the marketing game.

2. DESIGN FOR THE SCROLL-STOPPING EFFECT

In a world where people scroll three hundred feet of content per day (that's the height of the Statue of Liberty, by the way), your visuals need to stop thumbs in their tracks.[8] Research from Nielsen Norman Group shows that users only read 20–28 percent of the words on a page, meaning your visuals carry the heaviest load when it comes to engagement.[9]

A/B testing has repeatedly shown the power of bold colors, unexpected imagery, and contrast. Take Spotify's data-driven ad campaigns: By using quirky, high-contrast designs and humorous insights, like "Dear person who played 'Sorry' 42 times on Valentine's Day, what did you do?" they increased brand recall by 50 percent.[10] The formula? High-contrast colors, dynamic layouts, and authentic imagery beat stock photos every single time.

3. WRITE LIKE A HUMAN (EVEN WHEN YOU USE AN AI)

Marketers often fall into the trap of writing in corporate-ese, a language no one actually speaks. The best campaigns use conversational, snappy copy that feels like it was written by a human, for a human. Take MailChimp's famous "Did You Mean MailChimp?" campaign, which embraced humor and playfulness to increase brand awareness by 40 percent.[11] Or Apple's "Shot on iPhone" campaign that sparked millions of user-generated content posts.[12]

Shorter is often better—David Ogilvy's golden rule still applies: "Five times as many people read the headline as the body copy."[13] If your headline doesn't grab attention, the rest of your ad doesn't exist. Instead of "We offer innovative mortgage solutions," try "Buy a Home with 0% Down If You're a Veteran? Yep." See the difference?

4. MAKE DATA YOUR CREATIVE MUSE

Creativity isn't just an art—it's a science, and the best marketers treat it as such. Case in point: Netflix. By analyzing audience behavior, they create multiple thumbnails for the same show, dynamically serving users the one they're most likely to engage with. This micro-optimization increased viewer engagement by 20 percent.[14] Similarly, Meta's creative analysis shows that ads with people's faces perform 38 percent better than those without.[15]

So, test everything—colors, fonts, CTAs, and even the placement of a smiling face. Use AI-powered creative optimization tools to tweak in real time. In other words, let data fuel your creativity, not stifle it.

AI-POWERED CREATIVE OPTIMIZATION: YOUR COACH FOR BETTER CAMPAIGNS

The days of relying solely on intuition for creative decisions are long gone. Today, AI-powered creative optimization tools help marketers test, refine, and enhance their visuals and copy in real time, ensuring that every ad, email, and social post is data backed and performance driven. These tools analyze engagement patterns, user behavior, and design elements to recommend the best-performing creatives—often before a campaign even goes live.

One standout tool in this space is Persado, which uses natural language processing and machine learning to analyze emotional triggers in copy. Brands using Persado have reported a 41 percent increase in conversions just by adjusting their messaging to align with consumer sentiment.[16] Phrasee is another AI-driven copywriting tool that optimizes email subject lines, ad headlines, and social media copy, helping brands like Domino's and eBay achieve double-digit increases in open rates and engagement.

On the visual side, tools like Adobe Sensei AI and Canva's AI-powered design assistant analyze previous campaign data to suggest color schemes, font choices, and image placements that drive higher engagement. Meanwhile, VidMob is an AI-powered platform that analyzes thousands of video ad creatives to identify which elements—such as pacing, background colors, and facial expressions—lead to the highest conversion rates. A/B testing can now be automated and scaled, meaning marketers no longer have to guess which thumbnail, CTA, or Instagram Reel format works best; the AI tells you.

The best way to use these tools? Start by feeding them past campaign data to uncover insights on what's already working. Then let AI generate variations of ad creatives, test multiple versions in real time, and scale the highest-performing designs. As you will learn from eBay's case study in the next section, teaching the AI the company's tone, style, and audience preferences can be the difference between "spammy" and sincere.

When AI and human creativity work together, campaigns don't just perform better—they become unstoppable.

REAL-WORLD CASE STUDY

How eBay Used Phrasee to Transform Its Marketing Voice and Drive Clicks, Engagement, and Revenue

For more than two decades, eBay has been a giant in the e-commerce space, a marketplace where millions of buyers and sellers connect every day. With over 174 million active buyers worldwide and 1.5 billion live listings, the company was no stranger to innovation. Yet, when it came to optimizing its marketing language at scale, eBay faced a challenge even its most advanced algorithms couldn't solve: how do you create engaging, brand-consistent messaging for millions of email subscribers, without burning out your marketing team?

The Challenge: Finding the Right Words at Scale

With a subscriber base of over 101 million users across the US, UK, and Germany, eBay's marketing team was tasked with writing thousands of subject lines and email variations to capture customer attention and drive conversions. It was a process that required endless brainstorming, testing, and refining—a repetitive and mentally exhausting task for any marketer. Worse yet, while eBay experimented with AI-driven content tools, early solutions produced spammy, off-brand messages that felt robotic and impersonal, making eBay fearful that its distinct brand voice—and more importantly, its customer trust—could be at risk.

Still, the potential of AI-powered content optimization intrigued eBay. It knew that if it could harness AI the right way, it could scale high-quality, engaging marketing copy without sacrificing creativity or brand identity. Enter Phrasee, a company pioneering brand language

continued

optimization—an AI-driven approach that generates, tests, and refines marketing copy while staying true to a brand's unique voice.

The Solution: AI-Powered Language That Sounds Human (and Converts like Crazy)

eBay's partnership with Phrasee began in 2016, but not without skepticism. After previous AI failures, eBay's analytics team put Phrasee to the ultimate test: a rigorous six-month head-to-head comparison with another AI-driven content platform. Phrasee won the global contract, proving its ability to generate human-sounding, high-performing marketing language at scale.

Phrasee's team of computational linguists built a bespoke AI language model specifically for eBay. Unlike generic AI-generated copy, this model learned eBay's tone, style, and audience preferences, ensuring that every email subject line, push notification, and marketing message reflected the brand's personality. The results were almost instantaneous. Phrasee-generated email subject lines consistently outperformed human-written ones, leading to a 15.8 percent uplift in open rates and a 31.2 percent increase in click rates in the US alone.

And because Phrasee's AI continuously learns and optimizes over time, its impact didn't plateau—it kept getting smarter. What once took eBay's team hours of brainstorming could now be achieved in just five minutes per campaign, freeing up marketers to focus on strategy rather than sentence structure.

The Results: More Clicks, More Opens, More Revenue—and Happier Marketers

The numbers spoke for themselves. On average, Phrasee drove seven hundred thousand additional email opens and fifty-six thousand extra clicks per campaign. With such undeniable results, eBay expanded the AI-powered optimization beyond emails to push notifications, ensuring every touchpoint with customers was engaging, relevant, and conversion-driven.

But beyond the metrics, there was another surprising benefit: marketer happiness. As Gareth Jones, former CMO of eBay UK, put it, "Phrasee makes you money, so you're more likely to get your bonus." Not only did Phrasee improve performance but it also relieved the creative strain on eBay's marketing team, proving that AI isn't here to replace marketers—it's here to empower them.

Now, eBay and Phrasee continue to push the boundaries of AI-driven marketing language, optimizing subject lines, email content, and even on-site messaging. With AI as a permanent part of its marketing strategy, eBay has proven that when you get the words right, customers don't just click—they engage, they convert, and they keep coming back.[17]

THE PREDICTIVE PERFORMANCE PROTOCOL

What sets modern campaign optimization apart is the ability to anticipate and prepare for performance changes before they occur. According to research from McKinsey's Consumer Marketing Analytics Center, organizations using data-driven predictive optimization see a 25–35 percent higher ROI on their marketing investments.[18]

Netflix provides a compelling example of this approach in action. Their implementation of predictive analytics for content promotion campaigns yielded impressive results. For instance, if a user enjoys a particular genre or movie, Netflix suggests similar content, enhancing user engagement, leading to over 80 percent of streamed content being driven by these suggestions. This strategy has contributed to a customer retention rate exceeding 90 percent, surpassing competitors like Hulu (64 percent) and Amazon Prime (75 percent).[19] Additionally, Netflix's focus on original content, informed by data insights, has further bolstered subscriber growth and engagement.

Major brands have demonstrated how systematic implementation of optimization tools can drive significant improvements. Consider how Adidas transformed their campaign optimization process. They partnered with the platform Insider to enhance online experiences using AI-backed tools like Category Optimizer and Smart Recommender. This collaboration led to a 259 percent increase in average order value and an 18.8 percent rise in revenue per user within a month.[20] Additionally, Adidas utilized Criteo's AI-powered audience-modeling technology to expand their customer base in the Middle East and North Africa. This initiative resulted in a 66 percent improvement in ROAS for low-funnel campaigns and an 81 percent enhancement for mid-funnel campaigns over five months.[21]

FROM GOOD TO GREAT: THE AI-POWERED MARKETING TRANSFORMATION

The landscape of AI-powered marketing optimization represents more than just technological advancement—it's a fundamental shift in how businesses connect with their audiences and drive growth. From Sarah's real estate team leveraging multi-platform ad campaigns to Michael's comprehensive content calendars that establish omnipresent market authority, we've seen how AI transforms marketing from educated guesswork into precise, data-driven strategy. The integration of tools like Google's Smart Bidding, Facebook's algorithmic optimization, and LinkedIn's audience expansion capabilities demonstrates that success no longer depends on having the largest budget but on intelligently orchestrating AI-enhanced workflows that amplify human creativity and strategic thinking.

The most compelling aspect of this AI marketing revolution is its accessibility. You don't need enterprise-level resources to compete with industry giants. As evidenced by case studies from Press's 40 percent conversion increase with Meta's Advantage+ campaigns to eBay's transformation through Phrasee's language optimization, the tools and strategies outlined in this chapter provide a road map for businesses of any size to achieve remarkable results. This marriage of human creativity and AI efficiency is reshaping the marketing landscape, making sophisticated, high-performing campaigns accessible to David-sized companies ready to compete with Goliaths.

Implementation Blueprint: Your Ninety-Day Plan

PHASE 1: FOUNDATION (DAYS 1–30)

Begin with a comprehensive audit of your current tracking setup. This means reviewing all your analytics tools, ensuring proper installation of tracking pixels, and verifying that data is flowing correctly. Many organizations discover they're missing crucial data points during this phase.

Implement proper analytics by setting up the following:

- Goal tracking for key conversion actions
- Event tracking for important user interactions
- Custom dimensions for deeper analysis
- Cross-domain tracking if needed

Establish baseline metrics by gathering at least thirty days of clean data. This gives you a clear picture of current performance and helps set realistic improvement targets.

Set up testing protocols, including the following:

- Clear hypothesis documentation

- Statistical significance thresholds

- Test duration guidelines

- Result analysis frameworks

PHASE 2: OPTIMIZATION (DAYS 31–60)

Focus on platform optimization by implementing these elements:

- **Automated bidding setup:** Configure each platform's automated bidding features based on your goals (e.g., conversions, ROAS, etc.).

- **A/B testing implementation:** Start with simple tests (e.g., headlines, images) before moving to more complex elements.

- **Audience refinement:** Use platform data to create more targeted audience segments.

- **Creative testing:** Implement systematic creative testing using platform tools.

Establish cross-platform coordination through

- **Attribution modeling:** Understand how different channels contribute to conversions by setting up attribution models that match your sales cycle.

- **Budget allocation:** Distribute budget based on attribution insights and platform performance.

- **Message consistency:** Ensure brand messaging aligns across all channels while adapting to platform-specific best practices.

- **Performance tracking:** Implement cross-platform reporting to understand the full customer journey.

Attribution modeling deserves special attention here. Start with rule-based models like last click or linear attribution, then gradually move to data-driven attribution as you gather more data. This helps you understand which channels influence conversions at different stages of the customer journey.

PHASE 3: REFINEMENT (DAYS 61–90)

Advanced testing implementation means moving beyond basic A/B tests to multivariate testing, but only when you have sufficient traffic to achieve statistical significance.

Custom automation setup involves creating rules and alerts for performance thresholds, budget pacing, competitive monitoring, and anomaly detection.

Performance analysis should go beyond surface metrics to understand channel interactions, audience overlap, creative effectiveness, and cost efficiency.

Strategy adjustment should be based on comprehensive data review and focus on scaling what works, fixing what doesn't, identifying new opportunities, and optimizing resource allocation.

9

One to Millions: How AI Personalizes Marketing Like Never Before

Personalization is no longer just an enhancement in marketing—it has become the backbone of successful customer engagement. A staggering 80 percent of consumers are more likely to make a purchase when brands offer tailored experiences.[1] The modern consumer, whether in business-to-consumer (B2C) or B2B, is no longer satisfied with generic messaging. They expect brands to anticipate their needs, understand their preferences, and deliver content that speaks directly to them.

The challenge, however, is scale. It's easy to personalize a handful of emails manually or tweak ad copy for a small audience. But how do you create meaningful, individualized experiences for thousands—or even millions—of people across multiple channels? The answer lies in AI-driven marketing, where machine learning and automation work together to craft hyper-personalized experiences at scale.

The key to making this work is understanding which personalization strategies can be automated effectively without losing their human touch.

Here are five game-changing ways marketers can scale personalization across multiple channels, backed by AI-powered tools, case studies, and practical implementation tips.

1. AI-POWERED DYNAMIC CONTENT: THE ART OF REAL-TIME PERSONALIZATION

A fundamental mistake many marketers make is assuming that personalization is just about inserting a customer's first name in an email. Real personalization, the kind that drives higher engagement and conversion, requires delivering relevant content at the exact moment a customer is ready to engage. AI-powered dynamic content makes this possible by adjusting website experiences, email campaigns, and mobile content in real time, ensuring that every customer sees messaging that reflects their preferences, behavior, and intent.

But this approach isn't limited to e-commerce. B2B companies are also leveraging AI-powered dynamic content to enhance engagement. Platforms like Mutiny and Optimizely allow B2B marketers to tailor website content for each visitor, showing different case studies, testimonials, and calls to action depending on the company industry, job title, or past interactions.

The implementation of AI-driven dynamic content doesn't require an overhaul of your marketing infrastructure. Instead, tools like Adobe Sensei, Dynamic Yield, and Mutiny integrate seamlessly with existing platforms. Once activated, they analyze user behavior, historical data, and contextual triggers to determine which content variation will generate the highest engagement for each visitor.

The Content Customization Engine

The heart of effective personalization lies in dynamic content customization. Adobe's 2023 digital experience report emphasizes the growing demand for personalized content and the challenges organizations face in delivering it efficiently. Notably, 89 percent of senior executives acknowledge a significant increase in content demand, yet only 28 percent rate their organizations as good or very good at delivering content.[2] This highlights the critical role of AI-driven personalization in meeting content demands and enhancing customer engagement.

The key to successful implementation lies in sophisticated conditional logic. Here's how a leading retailer structures their dynamic content:

Conditional logic framework:

If [browsed_category] within last 48 hours:

Show [related_products] + [category_specific_offer]

Else if [abandoned_cart]:

Display [cart_items] + [limited_time_discount]

Else if [loyalty_tier] == "premium":

Feature [exclusive_preview] + [early_access]

Else:

Show [trending_items] + [new_arrival_boost]

REAL-WORLD CASE STUDY
How Synchrony Used AI-Driven Personalization to Boost Credit Card Applications

For decades, Synchrony has been at the forefront of financial services, offering credit solutions to consumers and businesses alike. But as digital banking expanded, the landscape grew more competitive, and customers faced an overwhelming number of options when selecting credit cards, financing programs, and savings solutions. The challenge wasn't just standing out—it was guiding each customer to the right product in a way that felt personal and intuitive.

Synchrony recognized that delivering a one-size-fits-all experience wasn't enough in the digital age. Customers wanted personalization, and they wanted it at scale. The company needed a way to use customer data intelligently—not just to understand what customers wanted but to tailor website experiences, product recommendations, and CTAs in a way that would drive higher engagement and applications. That's when they turned to Dynamic Yield, an AI-powered personalization platform.

The partnership focused on two key areas: home page personalization and user experience (UX) optimization. First, Synchrony integrated its data with LiveRamp, a data connectivity platform, to analyze customer behavior and segment audiences based on their relationship with Synchrony. Returning users saw tailored recommendations: If a visitor already had a furniture brand credit card, they were shown offers relevant to that brand rather than generic promotions. First-time visitors, on the other hand, were introduced to Synchrony's most popular or location-based offers to encourage immediate engagement. This personalization strategy helped increase home page engagement and improve discovery, leading to a 12 percent lift in CTR among cardholders.

But Synchrony didn't stop at just personalization—they also reimagined the UX of critical conversion pages. They identified a hidden opportunity in their health-care provider locator page, where visitors searched for medical practitioners. While these users weren't necessarily looking for financing options, Synchrony saw a chance to introduce its health-care credit card as a valuable tool for medical expenses. By experimenting with different CTA placements and messaging, they discovered that even subtle changes, like repositioning buttons, led to a 7 percent increase in credit card applications among nonmembers. Further UX tweaks, such as removing the distracting "Play Video" button from a home page banner, drove a 4.5 percent lift in application submissions for high-intent users.

This success illustrates how AI-powered personalization can simplify digital decision-making, improve customer journeys, and directly impact conversion outcomes in financial services.[3]

For marketers looking to get started with AI-powered dynamic content, a simple but effective prompt to use in AI platforms might be: "Create five variations of a home page banner based on visitor demographics, location, and past interactions with the website."

With the right tools, AI takes personalization beyond a simple name tag and transforms it into a real-time, adaptive customer journey—one that responds intelligently to customer intent rather than making guesses based on outdated segmentation.

2. AI-GENERATED, HYPER-PERSONALIZED EMAIL AND SMS CAMPAIGNS

Despite the rise of social media and instant messaging, email remains one of the most effective marketing channels, boasting an average ROI of $42 for every $1 spent.[4] However, the days of batch-and-blast email marketing are over. Consumers expect emails that are highly personalized, relevant, and timely—and AI is making this easier than ever.

Unlike human copywriters, who can only test a handful of variations, AI can analyze millions of data points and generate content that resonates with different audience segments instantly. The Phrasee–eBay case study earlier in this chapter demonstrated the power of hyper-personalized email campaigns.

Beyond email, AI-driven SMS marketing tools like Attentive and Postscript are helping brands send personalized text messages that feel conversational rather than promotional. By using AI to determine the right tone, urgency, and messaging style, brands can achieve significantly higher engagement rates.

For marketers implementing AI-powered email or SMS campaigns, an effective prompt for an AI content tool might be: "Generate an email subject line for a holiday sale that balances urgency and excitement without sounding spammy."

With AI handling the heavy lifting of A/B testing, language optimization, and delivery timing, marketers can focus on strategic campaign planning rather than micromanaging individual messages.

Advanced Email Personalization Framework: Beyond "Hello [First_Name]"

Email marketing has evolved far beyond simple name insertions. True hyper-personalization leverages AI, behavioral analytics, and real-time data to deliver contextually relevant and engaging experiences. Advanced email personalization transforms generic campaigns into high-performing, conversion-driven experiences. By integrating behavioral triggers, preference signals, and real-time data, businesses can create deeply engaging, relevant, and timely email interactions.

Dynamic Email Framework: The Core of Personalization

This section outlines the key components of an advanced dynamic email framework. This framework provides a structured approach to implementing advanced email personalization, ensuring relevance, engagement, and higher conversion rates across industries.

Implementing this framework will ensure that email marketing strategies are not just personalized but truly intelligent and predictive, leading to higher customer satisfaction and business growth.

Let's dive in.

1. Personal Context Integration

Emails should be context aware, incorporating real-time and historical customer data to enhance relevance.

- **Recent interactions:** If a customer recently visited a product page but didn't purchase, the follow-up email should acknowledge their interest and offer additional details, reviews, or a limited-time discount.
  - *Example:* A travel agency sends an email with flight options after a user searches for destinations in their app.

- **Browse history:** Track and utilize a customer's browsing behavior to suggest related products or content.
  - *Example:* An online bookstore sends an email recommending similar books based on the ones the customer recently viewed.

- **Purchase patterns:** Understand buying frequency, favorite products, and spending habits to personalize offers.
  - *Example:* A grocery delivery service sends personalized replenishment reminders for frequently bought items.

- **Support history:** If a customer recently reached out for help, follow up with proactive solutions, FAQs, or product tips.
  - *Example:* A SaaS company emails a customer who recently contacted support with additional troubleshooting steps and a case resolution update.

2. Behavioral Triggers

Emails should be sent based on user actions (or inaction) rather than arbitrary schedules.

- **Time of engagement:** Use AI to analyze when a recipient is most likely to open and engage with emails.
  - *Example:* If a subscriber consistently opens emails at 7 a.m., schedule future sends around that time.

- **Device preferences:** Optimize email content for the device a user most frequently engages with.
  - *Example:* A fitness app user who interacts mostly via mobile receives shorter, image-heavy emails designed for small screens.

- **Response patterns:** Adapt follow-up emails based on past email engagement, such as opens, clicks, and replies.
  - *Example:* If a user frequently clicks on discount offers but rarely on blog content, prioritize promotions in future emails.

- **Click habits:** Identify which CTAs and content elements users tend to interact with the most.
  - *Example:* A media company notices a subscriber frequently clicks on finance articles and adjusts their email newsletters accordingly.

3. Preference Signals

Emails should reflect customer preferences, allowing for deeper engagement.

- **Content interactions:** Track what types of content a user engages with and adjust future emails to match.
  - *Example:* A tech company identifies that a user prefers video tutorials over blogs and adjusts their email recommendations accordingly.

- **Feature usage:** In SaaS and app-based businesses, tailor emails based on feature adoption.
  - *Example:* If a CRM user has not explored automation features, send an email highlighting how it can save them time.
- **Communication style:** Understand whether a user prefers concise emails with bullet points or detailed breakdowns.
  - *Example:* A corporate learning platform allows users to choose between "Quick Updates" or "In-Depth Insights" for their email preferences.
- **Decision factors:** Analyze what drives customer decisions—price sensitivity, brand values, social proof, etc.
  - *Example:* A fashion retailer sends sustainability-focused messaging to eco-conscious shoppers while sending luxury-focused emails to premium buyers.

Implementation Tools: Bringing the Framework to Life

A strong personalization strategy requires the right tools for data collection, automation, and dynamic content rendering.

For data collection and integration: Segment.io

- Unifies customer data from multiple sources (website, app, CRM, and offline interactions)
- Helps track user behavior to power personalized email campaigns

For email personalization and automation: Customer.io

- Enables automated, behavior-driven email sequences
- Supports advanced segmentation to target users based on past interactions

For dynamic content personalization: Liquid Templates

- Liquid, an open-source template language developed by Shopify, allows for real-time content customization by enabling dynamic content insertion and logic within templates, making it possible to personalize messages and experiences based on user data or events.
  - *Example:* A travel site uses Liquid AI to dynamically insert destination recommendations based on a user's recent searches.

For real-time personalization: Custom APIs

- Fetches real-time data to personalize emails at the moment of send
  - *Example:* A food delivery app emails users with estimated delivery times and trending dishes in their area.

Implementation Example from a Fashion Retailer

Header: {dynamic_lifestyle_image} based on age/gender/style preferences

Subject line: Combines {weather} + {recent_browse} + {price_sensitivity}

Product grid: {behavioral_recommendations} + {size_preferences} + {color_affinity}

Offers: {purchase_history} + {price_sensitivity} + {loyalty_tier}

CTAs: {preferred_action_type} + {device_optimization} + {time_sensitivity}

Personal elements: {important_dates} + {milestone_rewards} + {loyalty_status}

3. AI-POWERED CONTENT AND PRODUCT RECOMMENDATIONS

Whether it's Netflix suggesting your next binge-worthy show or Amazon recommending products based on browsing history, AI-powered recommendation engines drive 20–30 percent increases in sales.[5] AI tools like Algolia, Salesforce Einstein, and Amazon Personalize allow brands to deliver highly relevant recommendations based on real-time customer behavior.

Retailers have been quick to embrace this approach. Amazon, for example, customizes nearly every element of its home page for each returning visitor, showcasing recently viewed items, recommended products based on past purchases, and even location-based deals. The result? Thirty-five percent of Amazon's total revenue comes from AI-driven recommendations.[6] Let's look at what Amazon's engine tracks to enable personalized product recommendations:

- Purchase Patterns
    - Category affinity
    - Price sensitivity
    - Brand loyalty
    - Purchase frequency

- Browsing Behavior
    - Time spent per item
    - Review reading patterns
    - Image viewing habits
    - Search refinements

- Life Cycle Stage
    - Account age
    - Purchase history
    - Return patterns
    - Review engagement

And here's how Netflix's recommendation engine works:

- Viewing Patterns
  - ° Genre preferences
  - ° Watching times
  - ° Completion rates
  - ° Binge behavior
- Contextual Elements
  - ° Time of day
  - ° Device type
  - ° Location
  - ° Day of week
- Social Signals
  - ° Household viewing habits
  - ° Similar user preferences
  - ° Rating patterns
  - ° Content sharing

For a B2B SaaS company, AI-powered personalization can suggest the next best webinar, case study, or white paper, ensuring that prospects engage with content that moves them further down the funnel.

A useful AI prompt for this might be: "Generate personalized content recommendations for a marketing executive of a health tech company interested in lead generation strategies to sell their software to therapists."

By leveraging AI-powered personalization, brands turn every touchpoint into a high-converting, tailored experience, ensuring that marketing never feels like marketing—it feels like a natural conversation with the brand.

REAL-WORLD CASE STUDY
British Retail Giant Scales Revenue
with AI-Driven Customer Experience

The British institution, Marks & Spencer (M&S), which has a heritage of over a century, built its renown on delivering an outstanding in-store experience, according to a case study released by Persado. Its employees built strong relationships with customers, intuitively understanding their needs and engaging them with the right words at the right time. But as the retail world shifted online, M&S faced a challenge: How could they replicate this personalized experience in the digital space? With a goal of achieving five billion personalized interactions and generating hundreds of millions in additional revenue, M&S needed a solution that could bring its customer engagement strategies into the digital age.

The Challenge: Cracking the Code of Digital Personalization

M&S had a major advantage: rich customer data collected through its popular Sparks loyalty program. But despite leveraging this data for product recommendations and promotions, there was still a missing piece: language. Traditional email campaigns and website content were performing well, but the company hadn't yet tapped into AI-driven emotional engagement to optimize how it spoke to customers across digital channels. The marketing team knew that words drive action, but without a scalable, systematic way to optimize messaging, they were missing out on potential revenue.

The Solution: AI-Powered Language
Personalization with Persado

Enter Persado, an AI-powered language platform specializing in Motivation AI—technology designed to understand what language emotionally resonates with customers and drives engagement. Instead of simply tweaking subject lines or ad copy manually, Persado's machine learning algorithms analyzed customer data and tested different emotional triggers to determine which words, phrases, and tones performed best.

continued

To ease the transition, M&S started small, focusing on high-value channels like website copy, email marketing, and static promotional content. One of the first tests? Email subject lines. By optimizing messaging with Persado, M&S saw an immediate 20 percent increase in order rates—a clear sign that AI-driven language was outperforming traditional copywriting approaches. As Persado's AI collected more data, it built a bank of insights, helping M&S understand what truly motivated its customers.

The Results: Higher Conversions, Deeper Insights, and Future Growth

The numbers spoke for themselves. Between June and December 2021, email conversion rates lifted by an average of 20 percent, reaching as high as 34 percent in peak months. But the impact went beyond just performance boosts. Persado uncovered deep behavioral insights that challenged common retail assumptions. For example, many retailers rely on urgency-driven messaging like "Only two left!" or "Hurry, before it's gone!" to push sales. But Persado found that M&S customers didn't respond well to regret-based language. Instead, they engaged more with messages that highlighted value, inspiration, and excitement.

With these insights in hand, M&S is now expanding Persado's AI-powered personalization beyond email, integrating it into web content, mobile apps, and push notifications. As the company continues its digital transformation, Persado estimates that at full scale, this technology could unlock tens of millions of pounds in incremental revenue.[7]

4. AI-ENHANCED CHATBOTS AND CONVERSATIONAL MARKETING

AI-powered chatbots are redefining customer engagement by providing instant, highly relevant responses tailored to individual users. According to Drift research, buyers increasingly expect real-time, individualized conversations with brands online.[8] This is especially crucial for businesses that operate globally, where responding to inquiries 24/7 would otherwise require a massive customer support team.

Retail brands like Sephora and Domino's use chatbots to recommend products, take orders, and answer customer questions instantly, creating a seamless shopping experience. In the B2B world, AI-driven platforms like Drift and HubSpot Chatbots are used to qualify leads, answer sales queries, and book meetings automatically. These bots use machine learning to determine which visitors are most likely to convert and tailor their messaging accordingly.

Implementing an AI chatbot doesn't require extensive coding knowledge. Most platforms come with pre-built AI models that can be trained using simple prompts. To help educate, convert, and sell using data-driven AI chatbots, you can go to chatbot.com to create your own chatbot.

As AI continues to improve, chatbots will evolve from simple Q&A machines to proactive sales and support assistants, delivering human-like conversations at scale.

5. AI-POWERED PERSONALIZED AD TARGETING

Digital advertising has always relied on audience segmentation, but AI is now making hyper-personalized ad targeting a reality. Rather than simply targeting ads based on demographics and interests, AI can analyze real-time behavior, intent signals, and micro-moments to serve the perfect ad at the perfect time.

For example, when Nike used AI-driven Facebook ads, it generated a four-times higher ROAS by dynamically adjusting ad creatives based on user interactions.[9] Similarly, LinkedIn Campaign Manager enables B2B marketers to personalize ad copy, images, and offers for different job titles and industries, improving CTR by over 20 percent on average.[10]

To get started, an effective AI prompt for ad personalization might be: "Generate three ad copy variations for a B2B LinkedIn campaign targeting marketing directors in the SaaS industry for [your product]."

AI-driven ad personalization ensures that every dollar spent on advertising is optimized for maximum impact, reducing wasted ad spend and increasing overall campaign efficiency.

BRINGING IT ALL TOGETHER: HERE'S HOW STARBUCKS DID IT, AND YOU CAN TOO

Starbucks has long been a pioneer in digital transformation, beginning with its app-based loyalty program in 2011. The program provided valuable insights into customer preferences, visit patterns, and purchasing behavior, helping Starbucks make data-driven business decisions. Recognizing the potential of AI, the company launched Deep Brew, a powerful AI platform designed to enhance customer experience and optimize operations. With over ninety million weekly transactions worldwide, Starbucks leveraged AI to personalize interactions and improve efficiency, staying ahead of competitors in the retail coffee industry.[11]

One of the key ways Starbucks utilizes AI is in personalizing customer experiences. Through its app and AI-driven personalization engine, My Starbucks Barista, the company gathers data on customer preferences, frequently visited locations, and past orders. This allows Starbucks to provide tailored recommendations, real-time promotions, and even inform baristas of a customer's preferred drink upon arrival. AI also plays a role in predicting consumer demand based on external factors like weather and seasonal trends, ensuring that promotions and menu offerings remain relevant and engaging for customers.

Additionally, AI helps Starbucks introduce new menu items by analyzing customer preferences and broader market trends. By identifying patterns, such as a preference for unsweetened tea or increased demand for cold drinks during heat waves, Starbucks can launch targeted products that resonate with consumers. These AI-driven insights have significantly boosted the company's ROI, with a reported 30 percent increase, alongside a 15 percent rise in customer engagement.[12] Starbucks' strategic use of AI has reinforced its position as a market leader, demonstrating how technology can drive both profitability and customer satisfaction.

By adopting AI-driven personalization, businesses can create more meaningful customer interactions, optimize operations, and drive long-term growth. The key to success lies in data unification, response optimization, experience coordination, and AI-driven business intelligence.

Remember, personalization isn't about technology; it's about understanding people. The AI just helps us do that at scale and with precision that wouldn't be possible otherwise.

AI-Powered Personalization Framework for Customer Experience

This framework provides a structured approach to implementing AI strategies for personalized customer experiences, based on successful models such as Starbucks' Deep Brew.

1. DATA UNIFICATION

Effective personalization starts with a comprehensive understanding of the customer. AI-driven platforms must unify data from multiple sources to create a single, cohesive customer profile.

Key Components:

- **Customer profile merger:** Consolidate customer data from loyalty programs, app usage, purchase history, website interactions, and customer service records into a unified profile.

- **Behavior tracking:** Utilize AI to track and analyze customer interactions across digital and physical touchpoints, identifying patterns and preferences.

- **Preference syncing:** Align customer preferences across platforms, ensuring consistency in recommendations, promotions, and interactions.

- **History consolidation:** Store and process past transactions, browsing behaviors, and feedback to refine future engagement strategies.

2. RESPONSE OPTIMIZATION

To maximize engagement, AI should determine the optimal way to interact with customers by considering their preferences, timing patterns, and content affinity.

Key Components:

- **Channel preferences:** Analyze data to determine whether customers prefer mobile notifications, email, social media, or in-store engagement.

- **Timing patterns:** Identify when customers are most likely to engage with offers and communications based on historical behavior and contextual factors like time of day or seasonality.

- **Content affinity:** Use AI-driven recommendation engines to personalize offers, content, and promotions based on previous interactions and inferred interests.

- **Device usage:** Optimize interactions based on device preferences (e.g., mobile app engagement vs. desktop browsing) to enhance user experience.

3. EXPERIENCE COORDINATION

A seamless customer journey requires coordination across multiple touch-points to ensure a consistent and engaging experience.

Key Components:

- **Message consistency:** Ensure that communications remain coherent across different platforms, reinforcing brand messaging and personalization efforts.

- **Timing orchestration:** Use AI to determine the best timing for customer interactions, aligning promotional campaigns and notifications with user behavior.

- **Channel handoffs:** Enable smooth transitions between online and offline interactions, such as linking digital orders with in-store experiences or allowing customer support teams to access app-based preferences.

- **Journey mapping:** Leverage AI to create dynamic customer journey maps that adapt to real-time behaviors and adjust engagement strategies accordingly.

4. AI-DRIVEN BUSINESS OPTIMIZATION

Beyond personalization, AI can enhance business operations to drive efficiency and revenue growth.

Key Components:

- **Inventory and supply chain optimization:** Predict demand patterns and optimize stock levels based on real-time and historical customer purchasing behaviors.

- **Dynamic pricing and promotions:** Use AI to adjust pricing and promotional offers based on demand, customer segmentation, and competitive landscape.

- **Operational efficiency:** Implement AI-driven automation for staff scheduling, in-store operations, and order processing to enhance customer service and reduce bottlenecks.

- **Location intelligence:** Use predictive analytics to determine the best locations for new stores or distribution centers based on traffic patterns, sales data, and demographic insights.

Implementation Road Map:

- **Data infrastructure development:** Invest in AI-powered data lakes and analytics platforms to unify and process customer data.

- **AI model training:** Develop and refine machine learning models for predictive personalization, leveraging historical and real-time data.

- **Integration across channels:** Ensure AI-powered personalization integrates with existing CRM, POS, marketing automation, and e-commerce systems.

- **Continuous learning and adaptation:** Implement feedback loops that allow AI models to evolve based on new data and changing customer behaviors.

- **Privacy and compliance:** Maintain strict data governance, ensuring compliance with data protection regulations while fostering customer trust.

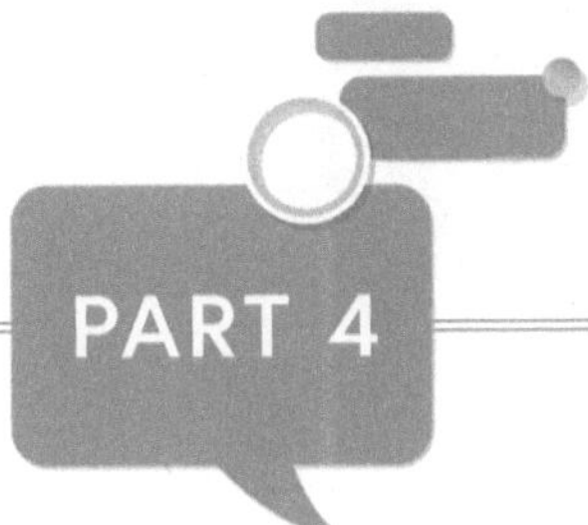

BUILDING SKILLS AND LONG-TERM SUCCESS WITH AI COACHING

10

The AI Accelerator: Fast-Tracking Skills and Mastery

According to McKinsey's 2023 workforce development report, organizations spend hundreds of billions of dollars globally on training, yet 70 percent of employees forget what they've learned within twenty-four hours of traditional training sessions.[1] This represents the growing gap between training investment and actual skill development.

Many businesses, such as Sarah's, feel as if they are stuck on the training treadmill. They conduct workshops, see temporary improvements, then watch skills slowly decline until the next training session. It can be exhausting and inefficient. Michael was similarly frustrated.

The breakthrough comes when you implement an AI-driven approach that transforms how your teams develop and retain skills.

THE SKILLS EVOLUTION REVOLUTION

AI coaching for skill building isn't just about making training smarter—it's about making it stick, scalable, and useful in the real world. Unlike traditional training programs that rely on one-size-fits-all approaches, AI coaching thrives on six key advantages that turn passive skill learning into active mastery.

1. PERSONALIZED PRACTICE SCENARIOS: THE AI THAT KNOWS YOUR WEAK SPOTS (AND FIXES THEM)

Imagine a golf coach that instantly knows you slice your drives to the right but never nags you about your already-perfect putting. That's AI in skill building. Instead of generic training modules, AI creates hyper-relevant practice scenarios tailored to individual gaps.

For example, in sales training, AI can simulate difficult client objections based on real call transcripts, forcing reps to refine their responses in real time. Research shows that employees forget 70 percent of what they learn within a day if they don't practice it.[2] AI ensures they get the reps they need—without wasting time on things they've already mastered.

2. INSTANT, PERSONALIZED FEEDBACK: THE AI COACH THAT NEVER SLEEPS (OR SUGARCOATS)

A 2023 study by McKinsey & Company titled "The State of AI in 2023" found that organizations using AI-driven coaching tools saw up to a 30 percent improvement in employee performance metrics. This enhancement was primarily due to the personalized and real-time feedback provided by AI, which allowed employees to continuously refine their skills and adapt to changing requirements.[3]

Unlike traditional coaching, where feedback is often delayed, vague, or sugarcoated to spare feelings, AI provides instant, data-driven guidance. Think of it like having a GPS for skill building: It doesn't just tell you when you've arrived; it reroutes you the moment you stray off course.

Take language learning: AI-powered apps like Duolingo don't just say "wrong answer"; they analyze the mistake and adapt future exercises to reinforce the weak spot. In corporate settings, AI sales coaches analyze speech patterns, tone, and pacing in real time, helping reps adjust before bad habits become permanent.

3. TRACKING BEYOND COMPLETION RATES: MEASURING WHAT ACTUALLY MATTERS

Traditional training metrics, like test scores and completion rates, tell you who clicked "Next" the fastest, not who actually learned something. AI shifts the focus to skill internalization by tracking patterns in real-world application.

For example, in customer service training, AI doesn't just track how many modules an agent completed—it listens to their actual calls post-training to measure tone improvement, empathy levels, and resolution effectiveness. AI even tracks micro-improvements, like reduced filler words or improved email response times, giving leaders a real-time pulse on skill adoption.

4. CAPTURING AND DISTRIBUTING BEST PRACTICES: THE ULTIMATE KNOWLEDGE MULTIPLIER

In most organizations, the best tricks of the trade stay locked inside the heads of top performers. AI changes that by analyzing these experts in action and distributing their best practices at scale.

For instance, AI-powered coaching in sales organizations records and transcribes top performers' calls, automatically identifying successful techniques (like mirroring a client's speech pattern) and incorporating them into training for others. This ensures that what works best doesn't stay siloed but becomes part of the organization's muscle memory.

5. EMOTIONAL INTELLIGENCE AND INTERPERSONAL SKILLS: TEACHING HUMANS TO BE MORE HUMAN

AI coaching isn't just about hard skills—it's about making humans better at being human. Emotional intelligence, negotiation skills, and leadership traits have traditionally been considered "unteachable" at scale. But not anymore.

AI tools now analyze facial expressions, tone, and word choice in real time to coach professionals on delivering more empathetic responses. In health care, AI-powered coaching tools help doctors improve bedside manner by flagging rushed speech or lack of patient engagement, ensuring a more compassionate experience.

A study at Stanford University explored the role of emotional intelligence (EI) in group work within science education. The research found that students with higher EI were more effective in navigating group interactions, leading to more equitable participation and enhanced engagement in scientific practices.[4] This suggests that fostering EI can improve collaboration and outcomes in educational settings.

6. MAKING SKILLS STICK: FROM TEMPORARY KNOWLEDGE TO PERMANENT CAPABILITY

Most training evaporates the moment people walk out of the classroom (or close the Zoom window). In fact, research on the "forgetting curve" shows that without reinforcement, we lose 90 percent of new knowledge within a month.[5] AI combats this by delivering micro-challenges at strategic intervals, ensuring knowledge is not just learned but fully embedded.

Think of AI coaching as the ultimate personal trainer for skill building: always available, never forgetful, and completely customized to what you need to improve. AI coaching reinforces learning through spaced repetition, gamification, and real-world application prompts. It doesn't just help people learn; it ensures they grow, adapt, and retain skills long after the training session ends.

AI COACHING IN PRACTICE

So, how does it work in real life, and how can you best get the promised advantages of AI coaching as described in the earlier section? Let's look at some of the use cases from the lens of Sarah and Michael.

SALES MASTERY

Sarah's journey with AI coaching began with a focus on luxury property presentations.

Sarah: I have an important listing presentation tomorrow. The clients are tech executives who've been very analytical in their research. How can I improve my approach?

AI Coach: Let's use the IMPACT framework . . .

I—Intelligence gathering

M—Market data preparation

P—Presentation structure

A—Analytical hooks

C—Confidence building

T—Technical depth

Let's start with your opening. How do you usually begin?

Sarah: I typically jump into property features and specifications.

AI Coach: Let's reframe that. Practice this opening . . .

Before we dive into the data, I'd love to understand what metrics matter most in your property decision. I've prepared detailed analyses of three key areas . . .

Sarah: That feels more consultative. But how do I handle technical questions?

AI Coach: Let's practice responding to complex questions while maintaining rapport . . .

1. Acknowledge the insight behind the question.

2. Provide data-backed response.

3. Bridge to emotional benefits.

Try responding to: "What's the home's power consumption pattern?"

Sarah: Great question—it shows you're thinking about long-term efficiency. The smart-home system has reduced power consumption by 34 percent compared to similar properties. You'll especially appreciate how it optimizes climate control during your morning meditation in the east-wing sunroom . . .

AI Coach: Excellent blend of data and lifestyle benefits! Let's practice handling ROI questions next . . .

The AI coach helped Sarah speak tech executives' language.

TIME MANAGEMENT MASTERY

Michael's journey with AI coaching took an unexpected turn when tackling his perpetual time-management challenges.

Michael: My calendar looks like a game of Tetris gone wrong. Help me regain control.

AI Coach: Let's analyze using the TIME framework . . .

T—Track current patterns

I—Identify energy peaks

M—Maximize focus blocks

E—Eliminate time waste

Walk me through yesterday's interruptions.

Michael: Constant client calls, team questions, and urgent email responses.

> **AI Coach:** I notice you're playing Whac-A-Mole with tasks. Let's practice the "Focus Framework" . . .
>
>   1. Power hours (Two-hour uninterrupted blocks)
>   2. Communication windows (batch similar tasks)
>   3. Buffer zones (planned flexibility)
>
> Role-play declining a nonurgent meeting:

> **Michael:** While this is important, I've dedicated this time block to client applications. Could we meet during my 2 p.m. communication window?

> **AI Coach:** Perfect! You've offered an alternative while protecting your focus time. Now let's design your ideal week . . .

The AI coach helped Michael understand that being available isn't the same as being effective.

LEADERSHIP DEVELOPMENT

Sarah leveraged AI coaching to enhance her leadership capabilities

> **Sarah:** How can I better develop my team while keeping up with my own responsibilities?

> **AI Coach:** Let's use the LEADER method . . .
>
>   L—Leverage strengths
>   E—Empower decisions

A—Assess progress

D—Develop skills

E—Engage regularly

R—Recognize growth

What's your biggest leadership challenge?

Sarah: I struggle delegating important client presentations.

AI Coach: Let's practice the delegation conversation. Role-play assigning a luxury listing presentation to your top agent . . .

FROM ZERO TO HERO IN SIX STEPS: HOW TO LEARN A NEW SKILL

Learning a new skill like content writing or copywriting can feel overwhelming at first—staring at a blank page, cursor blinking, silently mocking you. But don't worry, an AI like ChatGPT can be your personal tutor, editor, brainstorming partner, and even your simulated audience. The key is to treat it like a structured, interactive learning process rather than just asking it to "write something for me." Here's how to do it, step-by-step.

STEP 1: START WITH THE FUNDAMENTALS

Before diving into writing, you need to understand what makes good content engaging. Tell ChatGPT where you stand so it can customize the learning experience. Use a prompt like:

> I'm brand new to content writing and copywriting. Can
> you teach me the fundamentals step-by-step, including
> structure, tone, and persuasive techniques?

A well-trained AI will likely break it down for you, something like this:

Great! Let's start with the basics. Content writing is primarily
about educating, entertaining, or informing an audience, while
copywriting is more about persuasion and conversion. Both
require a strong understanding of the audience, clear messaging,
and compelling storytelling. Let's begin with structure. Most effective content follows a simple formula: headline → hook → body →
call to action. Now, let's try writing a basic blog introduction.

At this stage, follow up with:

> Give me a simple template for writing a blog post
> introduction that hooks the reader.

AI might respond:

Sure! Here's a simple but effective structure for an engaging
introduction . . .

1. Start with a hook—a surprising fact, question, or relatable
    statement.

2. Introduce the problem—what challenge does the reader face?

3. Promise a solution—explain what they'll learn or gain by
    reading further.

4. Now, let's practice. Pick a topic you're interested in, and I'll
    guide you through writing your first intro.

STEP 2: PRACTICE WITH AI FEEDBACK

Once you attempt a basic introduction, paste it back into ChatGPT and ask for feedback:

> Here's my first attempt at a blog intro. Can you critique it and suggest improvements?

AI might respond:

> Great start! You've got a solid hook, but your transition to the problem statement could be smoother. Try making the second sentence more emotional or urgent to keep readers engaged. Here's a refined version of your intro . . .

By repeating this cycle—writing, getting AI feedback, refining—you'll start to develop a feel for what works. Don't stop at introductions; work through full posts, social media captions, and persuasive email copy.

STEP 3: LEARN BY ANALYZING GREAT COPY

One of the best ways to get better at writing is to deconstruct what works. Ask ChatGPT to analyze strong examples:

> Give me a breakdown of why this Apple product page copy is so effective.

AI might respond by pointing out persuasive techniques like brevity, emotional appeal, and power words. Then, push it further:

> Rewrite this using a different tone—make it funnier or more urgent.

This exercise helps you understand how different styles impact readers and allows you to experiment with your own voice.

STEP 4: SIMULATE REAL-WORLD SCENARIOS

Theory is great, but application is what makes you a skilled writer. Use AI to role-play as a client or editor:

> Pretend you're my boss at a marketing agency. Give me a content brief for a product launch blog post.

AI might respond:

You're writing a 1,000-word blog post introducing our new eco-friendly water bottle.

- Target audience: Environmentally conscious millennials
- Tone: Friendly and informative
- Key messages: Sustainability, durability, and design
- Call to action: Encourage sign-ups for early access

Write the post and then ask AI to critique it from the perspective of a real-world editor. It will point out things like clarity, engagement, and whether the CTA is compelling enough.

STEP 5: DEVELOP SPEED AND EFFICIENCY

Once you understand the mechanics, push yourself to write faster without sacrificing quality. Challenge AI to help you outline content quickly:

> I need to write a 500-word article on "How to Start a Side Hustle." Give me a detailed outline.

This reduces the time you spend staring at a blank page. You can also use AI as a brainstorming partner:

> I need five engaging email subject lines for a fitness newsletter.

AI might respond with:

- Burn Fat, Build Muscle—Your 10-Minute Routine Awaits
- Struggling with Diet? These 3 Simple Hacks Will Help
- Transform Your Body with This 30-Day Challenge
- The Workout Mistake That's Costing You Results
- Science-Backed Fitness Tips You Can't Ignore

STEP 6: TRACK PROGRESS AND GET ADVANCED

Once you start improving, ask AI to help you self-assess:

> I've been writing for a month now. What's the next level? How do I refine my tone and storytelling?

AI might suggest studying advanced persuasion techniques like the Problem-Agitate-Solution (PAS) framework or the Attention-Interest-Desire-Action (AIDA) model. You can also start studying SEO and conversion copywriting.

For real-world practice, write and publish consistently—start a blog, contribute guest articles, or post on LinkedIn. Then, use AI to analyze your performance:

> Here's my blog post. Can you optimize it for SEO and suggest a more engaging CTA?

This step helps you transition from a beginner to someone who writes with impact and strategy.

By treating AI as your interactive writing mentor—constantly learning, refining, and experimenting—you accelerate your progress exponentially. The key is to use AI not as a crutch but as a coach. Over time, you'll develop instincts that go beyond what AI can teach. But by then, writing will no longer feel intimidating. You'll have a well-trained creative muscle that allows you to write engaging content on demand, whether it's a persuasive ad, an insightful blog, or an email that actually gets opened.

FROM NOVICE TO EXPERT: HOW TO IMPROVE A SKILL

Learning a new skill from scratch is certainly challenging. However, even improving a skill can be just as challenging.

Let's say you want to be a better negotiator. Learning to negotiate is like mastering a game of chess—except the board is life, the pieces are your words, and instead of capturing a king, you're trying to close a deal, get a raise, or at least convince your friend to pick the restaurant you like.

If you're someone who finds negotiating terrifying or ends up agreeing to things you later regret, don't worry—AI, specifically an LLM or a custom GPT ("The Negotiator"), can be your personal coach.

STEP 1: IDENTIFY YOUR WEAKNESS

Start by identifying where you struggle. Are you too quick to give in? Do you freeze when asked for a discount? Tell "The Negotiator" about your challenges. Try a prompt like:

> I struggle with negotiating. I either give in too quickly or
> avoid confrontation altogether. Can you teach me the
> basics of negotiation step-by-step, starting with simple
> exercises?

A well-trained AI will likely respond with a breakdown of negotiation fundamentals: anchoring, mirroring, tactical silence, and the classic "always ask for more than you expect." It might even start you off with a role-playing exercise:

> You are buying a used car. The seller is asking $10,000. You want
> to pay $8,000. How do you start the negotiation?

This gets you thinking and, more importantly, practicing.

STEP 2: PRACTICE, PRACTICE, PRACTICE

Once you get comfortable with theory, you'll want to practice in different scenarios. Ask your AI coach to act as a stubborn client, a skeptical boss, or a hardball vendor. Try:

> Let's role-play. You can be a hiring manager offering me
> $75,000, but I believe I deserve $85,000. Let's negotiate.

The AI might counter with:

> $75,000 is already competitive for this role. We have budget
> constraints. Why do you feel $85,000 is justified?

Here's where the magic happens. Instead of fumbling in a real-life scenario, you'll be able to refine your responses in a safe environment. You can try different tactics, highlighting your unique value, leveraging market data, or introducing nonmonetary benefits like remote work.

STEP 3: EVALUATE AND REFINE

Finally, evaluate and refine your skills. AI can help you analyze past interactions. Copy and paste an email negotiation you've had and ask: "How could I have handled this better?" AI will suggest improvements, tone adjustments, and even alternative phrasing.

If you're feeling brave, take it to the next level: Record your voice during a real negotiation and get AI-generated feedback. Over time, these micro-improvements add up. You'll go from avoiding negotiations to relishing the back-and-forth, all thanks to a tireless AI coach that never judges you (even if you start your pitch with "Uh, so . . . I was thinking maybe . . . if it's not a problem . . .").

THE IMPLEMENTATION FRAMEWORK

A study by Grant et al. found that both human and AI coaches were significantly effective in helping clients achieve their goals, with the AI coach performing comparably to human coaches over a ten-month period. The study revealed that a structured and systematic introduction of AI coaching features can lead to substantial improvements in goal attainment.[6]

As the study suggests, success with AI coaching requires a structured and systematic approach to implementing these capabilities in your organization. Companies following a structured implementation approach see much better results than those taking an ad hoc approach.

The implementation framework consists of three key phases: foundation, integration, and self-improving. Let's see how Sarah uses this framework.

Foundation Focus—Identifying Skill Gaps and Setting Clear Objectives

Before AI can coach effectively, it needs a clear understanding of where an individual or team currently stands. This phase involves mapping skills, assessing performance gaps, and prioritizing development areas using structured frameworks, like the Impact-Effort Matrix.

Sarah: How do we prioritize which skills to develop first?

AI Coach: Let's use the Impact-Effort Matrix . . .

1. Rate business impact (1–10)
2. Rate development effort (1–10)
3. Calculate ROI score (impact divided by effort)

What's your team's biggest challenge?

Sarah: Converting luxury property viewings to sales.

AI Coach: Let's break that into component skills . . .

1. Emotional intelligence in presentations
2. Technical knowledge articulation
3. Negotiation expertise
4. Objection handling
5. Follow-up mastery

Rate each for impact and effort . . .

At this stage, Sarah evaluates and prioritizes skills that deliver the highest impact with the least effort to generate quick wins.

Why This Step Matters

A 2021 McKinsey report highlights that companies with structured skills mapping see a 40 percent increase in training effectiveness compared to ad hoc learning.[7]

Real-world application: Top-performing sales organizations use AI to analyze CRM data and identify skill gaps that correlate with lost deals.

Integration Intensity—Embedding AI Coaching into Daily Workflows

Once priority skills are identified, AI coaching must be seamlessly integrated into day-to-day activities, reinforcing learning in real time. This involves

- Providing just-in-time coaching during real tasks (e.g., AI-assisted role-play before an actual client meeting)

- Using adaptive learning, where the AI personalizes the training path based on progress

- Analyzing real-world performance data (such as customer interactions) to fine-tune coaching

Here's an example:

Sarah: AI Coach, I rated "Emotional Intelligence in Presentations" as high impact but medium effort. What's next?

AI Coach: Great. Let's practice this in a real scenario. Imagine a client is hesitant because they feel the luxury home's layout is impractical for entertaining guests. How would you respond?

Sarah: I would highlight the spacious living areas and mention that other luxury clients have found the open layout perfect for hosting.

AI Coach: Solid answer! However, to make it even more effective,

- Acknowledge their concern: "I understand why that's important to you . . ."

- Use a compelling story: "One of my past clients had the same concern, but they found that . . ."

- End with an open-ended question: "Would you like to see how other homeowners have customized this space?"

Now, try again incorporating these elements.

Why This Step Matters

A *Harvard Business Review* study found that employees who receive real-time AI coaching improve performance much faster than those using periodic feedback. The study involved 139 employees at BCG and found that AI coaching helped employees learn skills 23 percent faster than expert-led workshops. Novices experienced 32 percent larger gains, and over half rated AI coaching higher than human instruction after only one session.[8]

Real-world example: AI-driven tools like Gong.io analyze thousands of sales calls, identifying key phrases that boost conversion rates, allowing reps to refine their pitches dynamically.

Self-Improving Coaching Systems— Creating a Learning Loop

The final phase ensures that AI doesn't just train once—it continuously evolves with each interaction, becoming smarter and more effective over time. This is done through

- **AI-driven pattern recognition:** Learning from previous coaching sessions to personalize recommendations

- **Feedback loops:** Collecting performance data post-coaching to refine future guidance

- **Behavioral analytics:** Identifying what techniques actually lead to improved performance

Weeks later:

Sarah: AI Coach, I've been using the emotional intelligence techniques you suggested. My clients are responding better, but I still struggle when they compare listings and say they want to "think about it."

AI Coach: I've analyzed the past ten client meetings where this happened. Here's a common pattern:

- Clients hesitate when they lack a strong emotional connection to a feature.

- You tend to shift into information-heavy explanations instead of emotional reinforcement.

- Let's try a response that ties emotions into decision-making:

  - "I completely understand. When you picture your ideal home, what does that look like?"

> ○ "I've seen other clients go through this same thought process. Can I share how one of them made their final decision?"
>
> Try this out in your next conversation, and I'll track how it influences your client engagement metrics.

Why This Step Matters

Studies from MIT Sloan indicate that AI-driven adaptive learning systems improve retention by up to 60 percent compared to static training models.[9]

Real-world example: AI-powered leadership training at Google analyzes employees' feedback on past coaching sessions to refine future training recommendations.

This framework ensures that AI coaching is not just a one-time training session but a living, evolving system that continuously improves performance. And according to *Business Insider*, organizations need to invest in upskilling and reskilling to prepare for AI's impact, highlighting the importance of continuous learning and system optimization.[10]

By implementing AI coaching with this structured approach, businesses can accelerate skill building, reduce training inefficiencies, and create high-performing teams that improve over time. And the best part? AI doesn't get tired of repeating itself—so you don't have to!

11

From Wishful Thinking to Winning: AI-Powered Goal Mastery

In the late 1990s and early 2000s, Ford Motor Company faced an existential crisis. Mounting losses, declining market share, and operational inefficiencies were threatening the company's survival. By 2006, Ford had lost \$12.7 billion in a single year—a staggering figure that signaled the urgent need for a strategic overhaul. Recognizing that fragmented decision-making and internal competition were impeding progress, newly appointed CEO Alan Mulally introduced a radical shift in goal setting with the "One Ford" strategy.[1]

The One Ford plan focused on breaking down silos within the organization, fostering collaboration, and setting unified, transparent goals across all global divisions. Mulally instituted a color-coded tracking system—green for goals on track, yellow for potential concerns, and red for critical issues—to ensure accountability in every department. This structured yet adaptable approach allowed Ford to streamline operations, cut inefficiencies, and improve market responsiveness.

The results were transformative. By 2010, Ford had returned to profitability, reporting a $6.6 billion profit, marking one of the most dramatic turnarounds in the auto industry. Notably, Ford was the only major US automaker that did not require a government bailout during the Great Recession. The implementation of cohesive, transparent goal-setting frameworks enabled Ford to align thousands of employees under a shared vision, reinforcing the power of strategic goal alignment in large organizations.

While financial growth remains a priority for most corporations, modern organizations are increasingly integrating sustainability and social responsibility into their goal-setting frameworks. A compelling example of this is Coca-Cola's 2015 sustainable business plan, a strategic initiative aimed at reducing the company's carbon footprint by 25 percent by 2020. Unlike conventional corporate sustainability efforts, Coca-Cola approached this challenge with a grassroots, employee-driven model that encouraged widespread participation.[2]

More than three hundred employees across various departments were actively engaged in brainstorming and executing sustainability strategies, ranging from water conservation initiatives to renewable packaging solutions. The company also leveraged data-driven AI models to identify inefficiencies in its supply chain and optimize distribution routes, leading to reduced fuel consumption and lower emissions.

By embedding sustainability goals into the company's operational DNA, Coca-Cola saw remarkable results. Within five years, it had already achieved a 20 percent reduction in greenhouse gas emissions, far outpacing initial projections. Moreover, the initiative boosted employee morale and engagement, with internal surveys reporting a 10 percent increase in job satisfaction among teams involved in sustainability projects.

KEY TAKEAWAYS FROM FORD AND COCA-COLA

Both Ford and Coca-Cola exemplify how strategic goal setting—whether focused on financial recovery or sustainability—can drive remarkable transformations. Ford's One Ford approach highlights the impact of organizational alignment and transparency, while Coca-Cola's sustainable business plan demonstrates how inclusive, purpose-driven goals can galvanize employees and improve brand perception.

For modern organizations, these case studies reinforce the idea that goal setting should not be a rigid, top-down process. Instead, businesses should embrace data-driven insights, collaborative input, and dynamic adjustments to remain agile and effective in an evolving marketplace.

The good news? AI can help with all this.

BEYOND NEW YEAR'S RESOLUTIONS

Sarah was reviewing her team's quarterly goals whiteboard, which had become what she now jokingly calls "The Wall of Good Intentions." Despite everyone's enthusiasm during goal-setting sessions, tracking and maintaining accountability had become about as effective as the average person's gym membership in February.

Michael faced a similar challenge with his loan officers' performance targets. He acknowledged that they had more tracking spreadsheets than actual progress. They were drowning in goals but somehow still treading water in terms of achievement.

Deloitte has reported that 58 percent of companies view their performance-management process as an ineffective use of time, underscoring the gap between goal setting and actual performance impact.[3] This represents the growing divide between goal setting and goal achievement.

The breakthrough came when both Sarah and Michael discovered an AI-driven approach that transformed how their teams set, tracked, and achieved goals.

DESIGNING GOAL-SETTING FRAMEWORKS

One of Sarah's agents kept setting the same goal every quarter: "Improve luxury property sales." That goal was about as specific as saying you want to get in shape while eating a donut. Their AI coach transformed the agent's goal into a precise pathway with daily micro-goals and clear success metrics. Within three months, his luxury property sales increased significantly.

Sarah's experience with AI goal setting began with a fundamental shift in how she approached objectives:

> **Sarah:** I need to improve our team's luxury property sales this quarter and need help with goal setting.

> **AI Coach:** Let's make this goal SMART using the LUXURY framework . . .
>
> L—Linked to revenue
>
> U—Unique market position
>
> X—Xcellence standards (metrics)
>
> U—Urgency drivers
>
> R—Resource requirements
>
> Y—Yearly trajectory
>
> What's your specific target?

> **Sarah:** We want to increase luxury sales by 30%.

AI Coach: Let's break this down . . .

1. Current luxury sales volume?

2. Average deal size?

3. Team capacity?

4. Market inventory?

Sarah: Currently $10M monthly, average $2M per deal, five luxury agents, fifteen available properties.

AI Coach: Based on this data, let's structure your goal . . .

Increase luxury property sales from $10M to $13M monthly by:

- Closing two additional $2M+ deals per month

- Converting 25% more luxury viewings to offers

- Reducing average days to close by 20%

Michael wanted to develop weekly milestones for his team's goals, so he utilized AI coaching to keep his team on track.

Michael: How do I ensure my loan officers stay on track with their targets?

AI Coach: Let's implement the TRACK system . . .

T—Target breakdown

R—Regular check-ins

A—Adaptive milestones

C—Celebration points

K—Key performance indicators

For each loan officer, we'll create . . .

1. Daily progress metrics

2. Weekly achievement markers

3. Monthly milestone reviews

Shall we design your first weekly check-in template?

Michael: Yes, I need something that maintains accountability without micromanaging.

AI Coach: Here's a structured check-in format . . .

Monday Progress Review . . .

*   Last week's wins (top three)

*   This week's priorities

*   Resource needs

*   Obstacle identification

THE ROLE OF GENERATIVE AI IN GOAL SETTING

These examples from Sarah and Michael show that when it comes to goal setting, GenAI can assist in crafting well-defined objectives, tracking progress, offering motivational reinforcement, and even predicting roadblocks before they occur.

Imagine a young entrepreneur who wants to scale her start-up but struggles with setting concrete milestones. By leveraging ChatGPT or CoachAI, she can break down her ambitious vision into structured, actionable steps. Instead of a vague goal like "grow my business," AI can refine it into "increase revenue by 20 percent in the next six months by implementing a referral program and optimizing digital marketing."

This ability to translate broad ambitions into clear, actionable steps is where AI's role in goal setting becomes invaluable.

A Framework for AI-Enhanced Goal Setting

To fully leverage ChatGPT in goal achievement, I propose the AI-Driven SMART+ Framework. This is an evolution of the classic SMART model—specific, measurable, achievable, relevant, time-bound goals— that incorporates AI's predictive and analytical capabilities.

Specificity with AI Refinement

Traditional goal setting often fails due to ambiguity. ChatGPT can refine broad aspirations into detailed, precise goals.

Example GPT prompt:

> I want to improve my fitness. Can you help me set a specific goal based on my current habits and lifestyle?

GPT output:

> Based on your current fitness level and schedule, a more specific goal would be: "Lose ten pounds in twelve weeks by following a high-protein diet and exercising for forty-five minutes, five times a week."

Measurable Goals via AI Analytics

One of the biggest challenges in goal setting is tracking progress. AI can help quantify goals and provide dynamic feedback.

Example GPT prompt:

> I want to improve my sales performance. How can I measure my progress effectively?

GPT output:

You can track progress using key performance indicators like lead conversion rate, revenue per client, and weekly sales growth. I recommend setting a 10 percent increase in conversion rates over three months as an initial target.

Achievability Through AI-Based Feasibility Checks

Many people set goals without considering their feasibility. GPT can assess whether a goal is realistic based on past performance, industry benchmarks, and personal constraints.

Example GPT prompt:

> I want to write a book in three months while managing a full-time job. Is this feasible?

GPT output:

Writing a book in three months while working full-time is ambitious. A more achievable plan might be writing 500 words per day, resulting in a 45,000-word manuscript in ninety days. I can help create a schedule to ensure steady progress.

Relevance Alignment with AI Insights

AI can ensure that the goals align with an individual's personal values, career trajectory, or organizational objectives by analyzing historical data and market trends.

Example GPT prompt:

> I want to switch careers from finance to digital marketing. What's a relevant goal for the next six months?

GPT output:

To make the transition, consider obtaining a Google Ads certification, building a portfolio with freelance projects, and networking with marketing professionals. A goal could be: "Complete three digital marketing courses and secure one freelance project in the next six months."

Time-Bound Structure with AI-Optimized Scheduling

ChatGPT can generate structured timelines and adaptive schedules to ensure goals remain time bound.

Example GPT prompt:

> I want to launch an e-commerce store in six months. Can you create a timeline for me?

GPT output:

Sure! Here's a six-month breakdown:
- Month 1: Market research, product sourcing
- Month 2: Website development
- Month 3: Branding and content creation
- Month 4: Marketing campaign launch
- Month 5: Beta testing and soft launch
- Month 6: Full-scale launch with customer acquisition focus

Plus AI-Powered Adjustments and Motivation

Unlike traditional methods, AI enables dynamic goal setting by continuously analyzing progress and suggesting modifications. If setbacks occur, GPT can offer motivational insights to stay on track.

Example GPT prompt:

> I missed my workout goals for two weeks. How can I get
> back on track?

GPT output:

No worries! Here's how you can reboot: (1) Start with three shorter
workouts this week instead of five, (2) find an accountability
partner, and (3) adjust your workout time to fit better into your
schedule.

THE MOTIVATION MOMENTUM MATRIX

The ability to maintain motivation over extended periods is one of the most challenging aspects of goal achievement. AI goal coaching offers an innovative solution, enabling sustained motivation by analyzing and reinforcing positive behavior patterns.

Recent research revealed in Deloitte's *2024 Human Capital Trends* report highlights that 63 percent of organizations identify long-term motivation as a critical factor for employee productivity but struggle to sustain it.[4] AI systems, by leveraging behavioral data, provide dynamic feedback and micro-rewards that help individuals stay engaged.

A particularly creative approach could be to use an AI-driven "motivation mirror." This system can translate individual performance metrics into personally meaningful rewards. For example, one agent who values travel can see her progress reflected in "vacation miles," equating closed deals to portions of a trip she aspires to take. Don't you think that will improve her motivation to hit the quota more often?

THE ADAPTIVE ACCOUNTABILITY ENGINE

Accountability is often the missing link in successful goal achievement. While motivation drives individuals to start, accountability ensures they follow through. AI can act as what I call the Adaptive Accountability Engine to provide personalized, dynamic accountability mechanisms that adjust to individual and team needs.

According to McKinsey's "State of AI in 2023" survey, teams that utilize AI to manage collaboration report a 35 percent improvement in project outcomes.[5] AI facilitates this through tools that provide real-time insights into team performance, identify potential bottlenecks, and suggest strategies to optimize group dynamics.

REAL-WORLD CASE STUDY
IBM—AI-Driven Performance and Workforce Management

IBM, a pioneer in artificial intelligence, has applied AI not only to its client solutions but also within its own workforce management. Through platforms such as Watson AI and internal digital tools, IBM has redefined how employees learn, develop skills, and receive performance feedback.

For example, IBM created AI-enabled HR applications like its Compensation Advisor, which uses Watson to help managers make fair and consistent pay decisions by analyzing employee data and market benchmarks. AI also powers "Your Learning," IBM's internal platform that personalizes training recommendations, links skill building to career opportunities, and integrates with performance evaluation processes.

This shift reflects IBM's broader move away from traditional annual performance reviews to a model of continuous feedback and

continued

data-driven insights. By embedding AI into HR and performance systems, IBM has improved transparency, enabled better talent deployment, and created a culture that connects learning with measurable business outcomes.[6]

TOOLS FOR ENTERPRISE GOAL SETTING AND ACCOUNTABILITY

Modern goal achievement requires selecting the right tools for your needs. First, you need to know what platforms are out there. Here's a comprehensive analysis of leading platforms.

Asana for Objectives and Key Results Management Capabilities

- Goal hierarchy creation (company → team → individual)
- Progress tracking with multiple view options
- Custom fields for goal attributes
- Automated status updates
- Integration with more than two hundred business tools

Best for:

- Teams of five or more members
- Complex, interconnected goals
- Cross-departmental collaboration

RescueTime for Focus Enhancement Capabilities

- Automatic activity tracking
- Focus session management

- Productivity scoring
- Website and application blocking
- Detailed reports and trends

Best for:

- Time-management goals
- Productivity improvement
- Focus enhancement

Notion for Goal Dashboards Capabilities

- Customizable goal templates
- Progress visualization
- Document integration
- Team collaboration
- Automation capabilities

Best for:

- Documentation-heavy goals
- Creative projects
- Team knowledge bases

Monday.com for Visual Goal-Tracking Capabilities

- Multiple view options (Gantt, Calendar, Kanban)
- Automation recipes
- Custom workflow creation
- Time tracking
- Advanced reporting

Best for:

- Visual project management
- Multiple team coordination
- Process-oriented goals

ClickUp for Comprehensive Goal-Management Capabilities

- Goal tracking at multiple levels
- Custom goal widgets
- Sprint planning
- Time estimation
- Workload management

Best for:

- Agile teams
- Complex goal hierarchies
- Detailed progress tracking

TOOL SELECTION FRAMEWORK

Selecting the right goal management and accountability tools requires a systematic approach that considers multiple factors. This framework can be used for tool selections for practically any need within your organization.

Start by conducting a thorough needs assessment of your organization. This means looking beyond just your current team size—consider your growth projections for the next twelve to eighteen months, as switching tools later can be disruptive. Evaluate your goal complexity, including how many levels of objectives you typically manage and how interconnected these goals are. For instance, a small marketing team might manage twenty to thirty concurrent goals with various dependencies, while a sales organization could track hundreds of individual targets that roll up to departmental objectives.

Integration requirements often prove crucial for long-term success. Examine your existing tech stack and identify must-have integrations versus nice-to-have connections. Consider both current and planned technology adoptions—a tool that doesn't integrate with your CRM or communication platforms can create significant manual work and reduce adoption rates. Additionally, assess your budget realistically, including not just the tool's cost but associated expenses like training, setup, and potential consulting needs.

Technical expertise available within your organization plays a vital role in tool selection. Some platforms require dedicated administrators or regular technical maintenance, while others offer more plug-and-play solutions. Be honest about your team's capacity to manage complex systems—a feature-rich platform that's poorly implemented often proves less effective than a simpler tool that's well maintained.

Implementation considerations extend far beyond the initial setup. Create a realistic timeline for user adoption, accounting for factors like team resistance to change, learning curves, and competing priorities. Map out training requirements in detail. Will you need different training approaches for different user groups? How will you handle onboarding new team members? Consider creating role-specific training materials and designating internal champions who can support the broader team.

Data migration and historical goal tracking continuity deserve special attention. If you're moving from another system, plan how to transfer existing goals and progress data. Even if starting fresh, consider how you'll maintain historical records for performance reviews and long-term trend analysis.

Success metrics should be defined before implementation begins. While improved goal completion rates might seem like an obvious metric, consider tracking more nuanced indicators. User engagement rates can reveal adoption success, while time saved in tracking and reporting often justifies the investment. Team satisfaction scores, particularly around goal clarity and progress visibility, can indicate whether the tool is truly serving its purpose.

Evaluate each potential tool against these criteria systematically, creating weighted scores based on your organization's priorities. Remember that the "best" tool isn't always the one with the most features—it's the one that best matches your specific needs while remaining within your implementation capabilities.

REAL-WORLD CASE STUDY
Cohere Saves Time and Increases Shipping Velocity with Centralized Knowledge

A case study presented by Notion describes how Cohere, an enterprise AI firm founded by former Google Brain researchers with Nvidia backing, has dramatically improved its operational efficiency by consolidating its workflows. The company estimates employees now save over seven hours weekly thanks to centralized documentation practices, based on Notion's research calculations. This transformation has enabled the organization to accelerate its shipping speed by 30 percent through a unified hub managing product development from start to finish.

The catalyst for this improvement was to address a fundamental collaboration problem. Previously, critical project details were fragmented across numerous platforms, creating communication breakdowns that forced teams into endless meeting cycles, Slack exchanges, and email chains simply to establish shared understanding. Product manager Ana Cismaru notes that universal visibility now makes cross-team discovery effortless: "Having everything visible to everyone at the company makes it so much easier to discover what other teams are working on and find natural points of connection."

Notion's synchronized block feature has been particularly transformative for Cohere's workflow. When launching new initiatives, teams can link information across their workspace so that any modification to critical details automatically propagates everywhere. This capability proves especially valuable when specifications change, removing the tedious burden of manually revising multiple documents. The result is a documentation-centered culture where employees access needed information instantly rather than hunting through disconnected systems or waiting for colleagues to respond.[7]

CHALLENGES AND CONSIDERATIONS IN AI-ASSISTED GOAL SETTING

Despite the advantages of AI-assisted goal setting, some challenges remain:

- **Overreliance on AI:** While AI can provide structure, human motivation and discipline remain essential.

- **Data privacy concerns:** Personalized goal setting requires sharing sensitive information, which raises security concerns.

- **AI bias in recommendations:** Since GPT relies on pretrained data, its suggestions might not always be perfectly tailored to individual circumstances.

To mitigate these, AI should be used as an enhancer rather than a replacement for human intuition.

THE FUTURE OF AI IN GOAL SETTING

The integration of AI into goal setting is still in its early stages, but emerging trends suggest a more personalized, adaptive, and predictive approach.

- **AI-powered habit formation:** Future AI models could analyze behavioral patterns to recommend habit-stacking techniques.

- **Emotional intelligence integration:** GPT could incorporate sentiment analysis to adjust goal-setting strategies based on emotional state.

- **Neuroadaptive AI:** AI could tailor recommendations based on neurological responses, optimizing learning and productivity strategies.

FROM ASPIRATION TO ACHIEVEMENT WITH AI

ChatGPT and other GenAI platforms are not just tools; they are digital partners in the journey toward success. By leveraging AI for goal setting, individuals and organizations can define clearer objectives, track progress effectively, and dynamically adjust to evolving challenges. The future of goal achievement is here, and it's powered by AI.

AI Is Not Just for Business Goals

Meet Emma, a thirty-two-year-old marketing professional with big dreams. She wants to travel to Italy, get in shape, save for a home, and improve her relationships—but like many of us, she struggles with staying accountable and tracking her progress. She sets ambitious goals every New Year, only to see them fade away by spring. This year, though, she's using GenAI, like ChatGPT, to not only set her goals but also track them, stay accountable, and, most importantly, achieve them.

STEP 1: SMART GOAL SETTING WITH AI

Emma starts by refining her goals with the help of ChatGPT's structured prompts. Instead of setting vague objectives like "I want to travel," she asks:

> I want to visit Italy in six months. Can you help me break this down into actionable steps, including budgeting and planning?

GPT output:

Step 1: Decide on travel dates and budget ($4,000 total, saving $667/month).

Step 2: Research flights and accommodations (set price alerts on Google Flights).

Step 3: Learn basic Italian (practice on Duolingo for fifteen minutes/day).

Step 4: Plan itinerary (list must-visit places and book tickets in advance).

By getting specific, measurable steps, Emma already feels more confident about her travel goal. She repeats this process for her fitness, savings, and relationship goals, ensuring each has clear milestones.

STEP 2: AI-POWERED GOAL TRACKING AND ACCOUNTABILITY

With her goals now well-defined, Emma needs to stay accountable and track her progress. Instead of manually updating a journal (which she often forgets), she uses AI-driven tools like

- Notion and ChatGPT Integration to create a goal tracker where she logs daily habits and progress

- ChatGPT as an accountability partner. She schedules weekly check-ins using the task reminder feature by prompting:

> ChatGPT, every Sunday, remind me to check my fitness progress, savings for Italy, and daily relationship habits.

GPT output (Sunday reminder):

Hey Emma! Time for your weekly goal check-in:
- How many times did you work out this week?
- Are you on track with saving $667 for your trip?
- Did you schedule quality time with your friends/family?

Let's celebrate your wins and adjust where needed!

This automated reminder system makes goal tracking effortless, ensuring she doesn't lose momentum.

STEP 3: AI AS A MOTIVATIONAL AND ADAPTIVE COACH

Life isn't always predictable. Emma encounters setbacks—unexpected expenses slow down her savings, and a busy work schedule disrupts her workouts. Instead of giving up, she asks ChatGPT for adaptive strategies:

I couldn't work out last week. How can I get back on track without feeling overwhelmed?

GPT output:

No worries, Emma! Let's ease back into it. Try 20-minute home workouts this week instead of your usual 45 minutes. Block time in your calendar for short walks after lunch. Small wins add up!

ChatGPT not only tracks progress but also adjusts the strategy when challenges arise, ensuring she doesn't fall into an all-or-nothing mindset.

STEP 4: CELEBRATING WINS AND ACHIEVING GOALS WITH AI

As months pass, Emma sees real progress—her Italy fund grows, she loses ten pounds, and her relationships feel more intentional. To keep herself motivated, she asks ChatGPT to create a visual representation of her achievements:

> Generate a summary of my goal progress so far and create a motivating message to keep me going.

GPT output:

Emma, you've saved $3,500 for Italy, completed 75% of your workout plan, and had twelve meaningful friend/family meetups. That's incredible! Keep going—your goals are turning into reality. Italy is just around the corner!

By using GenAI for goal setting, tracking, and motivation, Emma doesn't just dream—she achieves. AI ensures she stays accountable, adapts when needed, and celebrates progress, making personal growth more structured, engaging, and effective.

THE FUTURE

12

The Rise of Agentic AI: From Theory to Practice

The story of agentic AI begins with fundamental questions: What if artificial intelligence could do more than simply respond to our queries? What if it could anticipate our needs, take the initiative, and work autonomously toward achieving complex goals? These questions have driven researchers and developers to push beyond traditional AI paradigms toward systems that embody agency, or the capacity to act independently on behalf of users.

At its core, agentic AI refers to artificial intelligence systems that possess the ability to perceive their environment, make decisions, and take actions to achieve specific goals with minimal human intervention. Unlike conventional AI models that operate within strictly defined parameters and require explicit instructions, agentic systems demonstrate a degree of autonomy and adaptability akin to human problem-solving behavior.

THE HISTORICAL JOURNEY

The evolution of agentic AI emerged gradually through converging research streams. In the 1950s and 1960s, pioneers like John McCarthy, Marvin Minsky, and Allen Newell laid the theoretical groundwork for intelligent agents through their work on problem-solving systems and symbolic reasoning. McCarthy's development of LISP and his early articulation of programs with "common sense" represented early visions of what we now consider agentic capabilities. LISP was introduced by McCarthy in the late 1950s as a powerful tool for symbolic computing foundational to AI research.[1]

The 1980s and 1990s saw significant advancements in agent-oriented programming and multi-agent systems. Researchers like Michael Wooldridge and Nicholas Jennings formalized theories of agency in computing, defining essential properties such as autonomy, social ability, reactivity, and proactiveness. During this period, agent frameworks emerged that enabled software entities to monitor environments, reason about changes, and execute appropriate responses.[2]

A pivotal moment came in the early 2000s with the rise of web-based agents and semantic web technologies. Tim Berners-Lee's vision of a machine-processable web led to frameworks allowing agents to interact with complex information ecosystems. Companies such as SRI International developed precursors to modern AI assistants with projects like CALO (Cognitive Assistant that Learns and Organizes), which influenced Apple's Siri.[3]

The watershed moment for agentic AI arrived with the deep-learning revolution of the 2010s. Advances in neural networks, particularly transformer architectures, enabled AI systems to develop sophisticated language understanding, context awareness, and pattern recognition. This paved the way for agentic systems capable of nuanced instructions, context retention, and multistep task execution.[4]

More recently, between 2020 and 2025, the practical applications of agentic AI exploded. Large language models such as GPT-5, Claude, and others have accelerated development by providing powerful foundational models that can be augmented with agentic capabilities. Their ability to understand complex instructions, reason through problems, and generate coherent action plans has transformed the scope of AI agency.[5]

THE LATEST BREAKTHROUGH: CHATGPT AGENT AND BEYOND

In July 2025, OpenAI launched ChatGPT Agent, marking a revolutionary step in practical agentic AI. This unified system combines the capabilities of their previous Operator tool (which could click and navigate websites) with their Deep Research functionality (which excelled at synthesizing information from multiple sources) into a single, powerful agent that can handle complex, multistep tasks autonomously.[6]

ChatGPT Agent can now handle requests like "look at my calendar and brief me on upcoming client meetings based on recent news," "plan and buy ingredients to make a Japanese breakfast for four," and "analyze three competitors and create a slide deck." The system intelligently navigates websites, filters results, prompts users to log in securely when needed, runs code, conducts analysis, and even delivers editable slideshows and spreadsheets.

The agent is available to ChatGPT Plus subscribers, with Pro subscribers getting unlimited access. This represents the first time truly capable agentic AI has become widely accessible to everyday users.[7]

Meanwhile, Anthropic has advanced its own agentic capabilities with Claude 4 and the "computer use" feature in Claude 3.5 Sonnet.[8] These features allow the AI to control computers by taking screenshots, moving cursors, clicking buttons, and typing text—essentially using computers the way humans do.

CAPABILITIES OF MODERN AGENTIC AI

Contemporary agentic AI systems demonstrate capabilities that would have seemed like science fiction just a few years ago. These capabilities can be broadly categorized into several domains.

TASK AUTOMATION AND EXECUTION

Modern agentic systems can independently execute complex workflows across multiple platforms and tools. ChatGPT Agent can carry out tasks using its own virtual computer, fluidly shifting between reasoning and action to handle complex workflows from start to finish. It's equipped with a visual browser that interacts with the web through a graphical interface, a text-based browser for simpler queries, a terminal, and direct API access.

A practical example might involve an agent that researches market trends, compiles findings into a presentation, schedules a meeting to discuss the results, and sends personalized invitations to attendees—all from a single high-level instruction like "prepare for next week's strategy meeting."

INFORMATION PROCESSING AND KNOWLEDGE WORK

Agentic AI excels at gathering, synthesizing, and extracting insights from vast information landscapes. Unlike simple search systems, agentic knowledge workers can evaluate source credibility, reconcile contradictory information, identify knowledge gaps, and present findings tailored to specific user needs.

Anthropic's multi-agent research systems demonstrate this capability by using specialized subagents that work in parallel, with a lead agent coordinating their efforts. Their internal evaluations show that multi-agent systems outperformed single-agent systems by 90.2 percent on research tasks, particularly excelling at breadth-first queries that involve pursuing multiple independent directions simultaneously.[9]

REASONING AND PROBLEM-SOLVING

Perhaps the most impressive capability of modern agentic systems is their ability to engage in multistep reasoning processes. These systems can break down complex problems, explore solution paths, evaluate trade-offs, and justify their decisions with logical arguments.

ChatGPT Agent demonstrates state-of-the-art performance on Humanity's Last Exam, scoring 41.6 percent on a challenging test comprising thousands of questions across more than one hundred subjects—a new benchmark for AI reasoning capabilities.[10]

CREATIVE AND CONTENT PRODUCTION

Agentic AI has revolutionized creative workflows by understanding not just individual tasks but entire creative processes. Modern agents can maintain narrative coherence across long-form content, adapt to feedback in real time, and resolve creative challenges independently.

ChatGPT Agent's creative capabilities extend beyond individual content generation to orchestrating entire creative workflows. When deployed for complex content production tasks, the system can autonomously coordinate multiple specialized processes—from research and ideation to drafting and refinement—demonstrating how agentic AI can manage end-to-end creative pipelines while maintaining consistency and quality across all deliverables.

LEARNING AND ADAPTATION

Unlike static systems with fixed capabilities, agentic AI can improve through experience and feedback. Modern agents can identify patterns in user interactions, refine their understanding of user preferences, adapt to changing environments, and transfer knowledge across domains.

ChatGPT Agent is designed for iterative, collaborative workflows, allowing users to interrupt at any point to clarify instructions or change the task entirely. The agent picks up where it left off with new information while retaining previous progress.

REAL-WORLD APPLICATIONS AND CASE STUDIES

The transition of agentic AI from research laboratories to practical applications has been remarkably swift. Here are some notable real-world implementations across various industries.

BUSINESS PROCESS AUTOMATION

Companies like Trellix use Claude to triage and investigate security issues, while Block has built an agent that allows nontechnical staff to access its data systems using natural language, saving engineers significant time.[11]

CONTENT MARKETING AND DIGITAL STRATEGY

One of the most transformative applications of agentic AI lies in content marketing and digital strategy. Modern agents can now handle entire content marketing workflows with minimal human intervention, revolutionizing how businesses approach their digital presence. Here is how an agentic AI system can help with some of the key content marketing and digital strategy tasks:

- **Research and strategy development:** Agentic systems can autonomously research target audiences, analyze competitor strategies, identify trending topics, and develop comprehensive content strategies. They can scan social media platforms, analyze engagement metrics, and identify content gaps in the market.

- **Content creation pipeline:** A specialized content creation agent can generate blog posts, social media content, email campaigns, and video scripts while maintaining brand voice consistency. These agents understand SEO principles, incorporate relevant keywords naturally, and adapt content for different platforms and audiences.

- **Multi-platform content adaptation:** From a single piece of source content, agents can automatically create platform-specific variations—turning a blog post into Twitter threads, LinkedIn articles, Instagram captions, and YouTube descriptions, each optimized for the platform's unique requirements and audience expectations.

- **SEO and analytics integration:** Advanced agents continuously monitor search trends, analyze keyword performance, and automatically optimize content for search engines. They can track content performance across multiple platforms, identify what resonates with audiences, and adjust future content strategies accordingly.

- **Email marketing automation:** Agentic systems can segment audiences, personalize email content, optimize send times, and conduct A/B testing automatically. They analyze open rates, click-through rates, and conversion metrics to continuously improve campaign performance.

SCIENTIFIC DISCOVERY AND RESEARCH

Companies like Asana, Canva, Cognition, DoorDash, Replit, and The Browser Company are exploring agentic capabilities for tasks requiring dozens or even hundreds of steps to complete. For example, Replit uses Claude 3.5 Sonnet's computer use capabilities to develop features that evaluate apps as they're being built.[12]

In pharmaceutical research, agentic AI systems are accelerating drug discovery by automatically designing experiments, analyzing molecular interactions, and predicting potential therapeutic compounds. These systems can work continuously, exploring thousands of possibilities that would take human researchers months to investigate.[13]

CUSTOMER SERVICE AND SUPPORT

Modern customer service agents can handle complex, multistep support requests by accessing multiple systems, understanding context from previous interactions, and providing personalized solutions. They can escalate issues appropriately, schedule follow-ups, and even proactively reach out to customers based on usage patterns or potential issues.

CREATING YOUR OWN AI AGENTS: A NO-CODE APPROACH

While the preceding examples represent cutting-edge implementations, the democratization of AI tools has made it possible for individuals and small businesses to create their own agentic systems without any technical expertise. Here's a comprehensive guide to building your first AI agent using accessible, no-code tools.

STEP 1: DEFINE YOUR AGENT'S PURPOSE AND SCOPE

Every effective agent begins with a clear definition of its purpose. Rather than creating a general-purpose assistant, focus on a specific domain or task where an agent could provide meaningful value. Consider:

- What specific problem will your agent solve?
- What information and tools will it need access to?
- What would success look like for this agent?
- What constraints or limitations should the agent operate within?

For example, you might create an agent that manages your social media presence by monitoring brand mentions, scheduling posts, responding to comments, and generating weekly performance reports. The more specific your definition, the more effective your agent will be.

STEP 2: CHOOSE YOUR PLATFORM

Several platforms now offer accessible entry points for creating agentic systems without requiring any coding knowledge.

ChatGPT Custom GPTs

Custom GPTs provide the most straightforward way to create specialized agents. With ChatGPT Agent now available, users can create sophisticated agents that can browse the web, analyze files, and perform complex tasks.

To create a custom GPT, follow these steps:

1. Visit chat.openai.com and log in to your account.

2. Click "Explore" in the sidebar and select "Create a GPT."

3. Define your agent's role, capabilities, and limitations through natural language instructions.

4. Upload reference materials (documents, spreadsheets, etc.) that your agent should use.

5. Configure settings like web browsing and file analysis capabilities.

Workflow Automation Platforms

For more complex multistep processes, workflow automation platforms offer powerful visual builders for creating agentic systems.

n8n

n8n is a free and open-source workflow automation platform that uniquely combines AI capabilities with business process automation. It offers the flexibility of code with the speed of no-code, allowing users to create agentic systems on a single screen and integrate any LLM into workflows through drag-and-drop interface.

n8n's library includes more than six thousand community-built templates for AI workflows, making it easy for beginners to get started. The platform allows users to build agents that can make decisions, interact with apps, and execute tasks without constant human input.

Zapier

Zapier's simple and intuitive interface makes it accessible to users with no technical background. The platform now includes AI features that can intelligently extract and transform data, generate workflows using natural language prompts, and diagnose errors in plain language.

Make (Formerly Integromat)

Make provides a versatile visual platform with a drag-and-drop interface for creating workflows by connecting modules representing different apps and actions. It offers AI integrations, allowing connection to platforms like OpenAI, Anthropic Claude, and Hugging Face.

STEP 3: DESIGN YOUR AGENT'S WORKFLOW

The power of agentic AI lies in its ability to handle multistep processes autonomously. When designing your agent's workflow, think in terms of triggers, conditions, and actions:

Triggers: What events will activate your agent? This could be receiving an email, a scheduled time, a new social media mention, or a form submission on your website.

Conditions: What logic should your agent follow? For example, "If the email is from a VIP customer, prioritize it" or "If the social media mention is negative, alert the PR team."

Actions: What specific tasks should your agent perform? This might include sending responses, updating databases, creating calendar events, or generating reports.

Example: Social Media Management Agent

1. **Trigger:** New mention of your brand on social media

2. **Conditions:**
   - If sentiment is positive → Like and share
   - If sentiment is negative → Alert team and draft diplomatic response
   - If it's a question → Research answer from the knowledge base

3. **Actions:**
   - Respond appropriately
   - Log interaction in CRM
   - Update sentiment tracking dashboard

STEP 4: INTEGRATE YOUR TOOLS AND DATA SOURCES

Modern agentic systems become powerful through integration with existing tools and data sources. Most no-code platforms offer extensive integration libraries.

Essential Integrations for Business Agents

- Communication: Email (Gmail, Outlook), Slack, Microsoft Teams
- Document storage: Google Drive, Dropbox, OneDrive
- Customer management: Salesforce, HubSpot, Airtable
- Social media: Twitter, LinkedIn, Facebook, Instagram
- Analytics: Google Analytics, social media analytics platforms
- E-commerce: Shopify, WooCommerce, Amazon

Data Sources to Consider

- Customer databases and CRM systems

- Product catalogs and inventory systems

- Financial data and accounting software

- Website analytics and performance metrics

- Social media engagement data

STEP 5: IMPLEMENT FEEDBACK AND LEARNING MECHANISMS

Effective agents improve through feedback and iteration. Most platforms provide analytics and monitoring capabilities to track your agent's performance.

Key Metrics to Monitor

- Task completion rates

- Response accuracy

- User satisfaction scores

- Processing time

- Error rates

Continuous Improvement Strategies

- Regular review of agent logs and outputs

- A/B testing different approaches

- User feedback collection

- Performance metric analysis

- Regular updates to knowledge bases and instructions

STEP 6: IMPLEMENT SAFEGUARDS AND QUALITY CONTROL

Responsible agent development requires appropriate guardrails to ensure reliable and safe operation. The autonomous nature of agentic AI makes this step particularly crucial, as poorly designed agents can cause significant problems when operating without direct supervision.

Clear scope boundaries represent the first line of defense against agent overreach. Your agent should understand precisely what it can and cannot do, and it should have explicit instructions about when to seek human input. For example, a customer service agent might handle routine inquiries about shipping and returns but escalate complex technical issues or complaints to human representatives. This prevents the agent from providing incorrect information or making promises the company cannot keep.

Human approval requirements become essential for high-stakes decisions that could significantly impact your business or customers. A marketing agent might automatically schedule social media posts and respond to comments, but it should require human approval before launching expensive advertising campaigns or responding to PR crises. The key is identifying which decisions carry enough risk to warrant human oversight without slowing down routine operations.

Confidence indicators help users understand when agent responses might be uncertain or speculative. Modern AI systems can assess their own confidence levels and communicate this to users through phrases like "I'm not completely certain about this" or "This recommendation is based on limited data." This transparency helps users make informed decisions about whether to trust the agent's output or seek additional verification.

Error handling and fallback procedures ensure your agent can gracefully handle unexpected situations. When an agent encounters a task it cannot complete or information it cannot find, it should have clear protocols for what to do next. This might involve notifying a human operator, suggesting alternative approaches, or providing partial results with explanations about what could not be completed.

Regular monitoring and oversight remain necessary even for well-designed agents. This includes reviewing agent logs to identify patterns in errors or unexpected behaviors, tracking performance metrics over time, and conducting periodic audits of agent decisions and outputs. Many businesses schedule weekly reviews of their agents' activities to catch issues early and identify opportunities for improvement.

THE FUTURE OF WORK WITH AGENTIC AI

The integration of agentic AI into the workplace represents one of the most significant shifts in management and organizational structure since the industrial revolution. As AI agents become capable colleagues rather than mere tools, managers and leaders must develop entirely new frameworks for overseeing hybrid teams of human and digital workers.

Managing digital employees requires fundamentally different approaches than traditional human resource management. Unlike human workers who need motivation, career development, and emotional support, AI agents require performance monitoring, capability optimization, and strategic alignment with organizational objectives. Managers must learn to evaluate agent productivity not just in terms of task completion but also in terms of decision quality, resource efficiency, and adaptation to changing circumstances. This involves understanding metrics like token consumption rates, error patterns, and learning curves that have no equivalent in human performance management.

The concept of team dynamics takes on new dimensions when AI agents join human workforces. Human employees must learn to collaborate effectively with agents that may process information faster but lack the emotional intelligence and contextual understanding that come naturally to humans. Successful teams will leverage the complementary strengths of both human and artificial intelligence—using agents for data processing, pattern recognition, and routine decision-making while relying on humans for creative problem-solving, relationship management, and strategic thinking. Managers must facilitate this collaboration by clearly defining roles and establishing communication protocols. They should also ensure that both human and AI team members understand their contributions to shared objectives.

The career development landscape will also transform as workers learn to augment their capabilities through AI collaboration rather than competing with automation. Forward-thinking organizations are already training employees to work effectively with AI agents by developing skills in prompt engineering, AI output evaluation, and human–AI work-flow design. These competencies are becoming as essential as traditional technical skills, and they require ongoing investment in education and professional development.

Workers who master human–AI collaboration will find themselves more valuable and productive, while those who resist adaptation may find their roles increasingly marginalized.

13

From Resistance to Renaissance

Sarah sat in her office reading an email from one of her veteran agents that might as well have been written in all caps with multiple exclamation points. The message was clear: "I've been selling houses for twenty years without AI, and I don't need a robot to tell me how to do my job!"

Meanwhile, Michael was facing resistance too. One of his most experienced loan officers had dubbed their new AI coaching system "HAL 9000's Annoying Cousin" and was stubbornly clinging to his paper-based processes like a captain going down with a particularly disorganized ship.

A 2024 report by the World Economic Forum revealed that 58 percent of employees hesitate to embrace AI tools due to concerns about data privacy and their ability to adapt.[1] This represents a vast chasm between AI's potential and people's willingness to embrace it.

THE THREAT TRIFECTA

What makes overcoming AI resistance particularly challenging is what I've identified as the Threat Trifecta: the three core fears that fuel resistance to AI adoption.

First, there's what I call the Replacement Reflex, the deep-seated fear that AI will make human expertise obsolete. Surveys indicate that nearly half of professionals worry about AI replacing their jobs, with some even hiding their use of AI tools out of fear it will make them appear dispensable to employers.[2] This job substitution fear is reinforced in sectors where AI-driven automation streamlines or eliminates previously human-dependent roles, directly threatening job security and life satisfaction, especially where tasks are repetitive or routinized.

Second, we encounter the Competence Concern, the worry that learning new AI systems will expose skill gaps. Michael's team faced this head-on when implementing their new AI coaching system. The Competence Concern fuels resistance: Employees often experience anxiety about being exposed as unprepared or lacking the technical skills needed to thrive in an AI-enhanced environment. Recent studies highlight that only 39 percent of workers using AI have received formal training, while 77 percent believe AI will have a profound impact on their careers, intensifying the perception of a widening skills gap and amplifying discomfort with learning new technologies.[3] These intertwined fears create powerful psychological and organizational roadblocks, making successful AI adoption not just a technical but fundamentally a human challenge.

Third, there's the Control Conundrum, or the fear of losing autonomy to AI systems. Just as people want to control their home temperature using a thermostat, people want to control their work processes. They need to see that AI is more like a smart thermostat, enhancing their control, not taking it away.

The solution to overcome the Threat Trifecta lies in what I've developed as the Trust Triangle: a three-pronged approach to building confidence in AI systems. Understanding and addressing these fears requires a proactive approach that combines clear communication, transparent policies, and consistent education.

Organizations that tackle the Threat Trifecta head-on are better positioned to build trust and foster adoption of AI coaching systems.

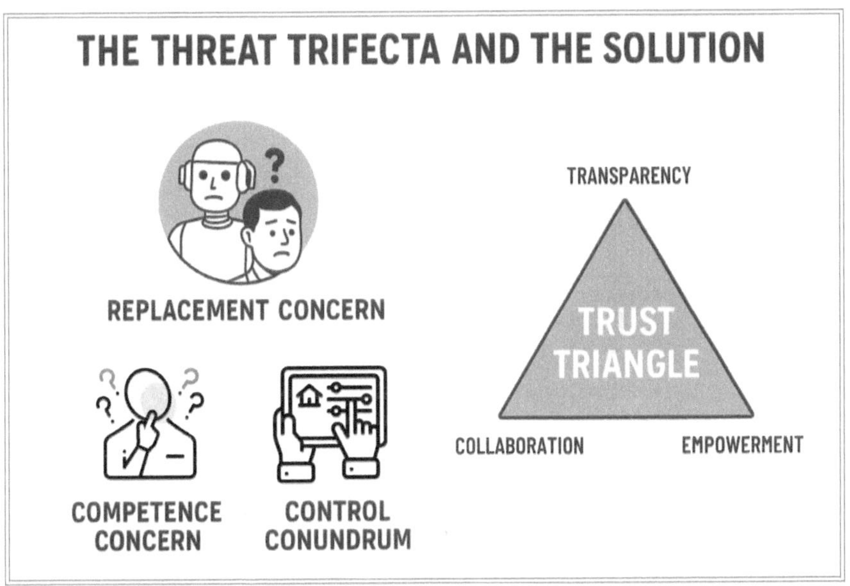

THE TRUST TRIANGLE

Building trust is critical for overcoming resistance to AI coaching. The Trust Triangle provides a structured framework to establish confidence in AI systems by focusing on three pillars: transparency, collaboration, and empowerment.

1. **Transparency**: Organizations must clearly communicate how AI systems operate, what data is being used, and for what purpose. For example, Salesforce provides detailed documentation and live Q&A sessions to address employee concerns about its AI tools, which has resulted in higher adoption rates.[4]

2. **Collaboration**: By involving employees in the development and implementation of AI systems, organizations can ensure the tools meet user needs. Spotify fosters collaboration by organizing autonomous, cross-functional squads that continuously incorporate feedback from both employees and stakeholders. This iterative approach ensures the development of user-centric AI tools and features that better meet employee needs, build trust, and facilitate smoother adoption across the organization.[5]

3. **Empowerment**: AI tools should be positioned as enablers that amplify human potential. Coursera's AI-powered Coach acts as a personalized learning assistant that empowers users to take control of their development journey. It provides tailored guidance, interactive feedback, and motivational support, helping learners stay on track, build mastery, and achieve their individual learning goals.[6]

These pillars create a culture of trust where employees feel valued, informed, and supported, paving the way for successful AI adoption.

THE SUCCESS STORY SYNDROME

One of the subtle barriers to adopting AI coaching is what I call the "Success Story Syndrome," where organizations and individuals overly rely on curated narratives of AI triumphs. These polished tales—often highlighted in marketing materials or industry case studies—showcase AI as a magical solution, delivering quick and effortless results. While inspiring, these stories often gloss over the challenges of implementation, adaptation, and cultural shifts required to make AI coaching work. This can lead to unrealistic expectations and, paradoxically, resistance when reality fails to match the idealized vision.

The syndrome also creates a narrow view of what success with AI looks like. Organizations may try to replicate strategies from these success stories without considering their unique context, resources, or readiness. When outcomes deviate from these benchmarks, it can breed skepticism about AI's effectiveness, reinforcing resistance instead of fostering trust. Additionally, by focusing exclusively on successes, these narratives often ignore the incremental progress, failures, and learning curves that are integral to long-term AI adoption.

To overcome the Success Story Syndrome, organizations must emphasize transparency and diversity in their narratives. Highlighting not just successes but also the challenges and iterative learning involved can provide a more balanced perspective. By framing AI as a tool for continuous improvement rather than instant transformation, organizations can set realistic expectations and build a culture of experimentation and growth, easing resistance to adoption.

REAL-WORLD CASE STUDY
How Airbus Overcame the Success Story Syndrome

Initially, Airbus was influenced by the growing hype around AI and machine learning, expecting rapid results by implementing advanced analytics and AI in manufacturing and operations. However, they quickly encountered setbacks—data inconsistencies, lack of alignment

continued

between engineering and data science teams, and overestimated expectations about how easily AI could be embedded into complex aerospace systems.

Instead of framing AI as an overnight revolution, Airbus recalibrated. They launched the *Skywise* platform, not just as a flashy data tool but as an open ecosystem for iterative collaboration. Importantly, they invested in change management: aligning stakeholders, ensuring data governance, and building a learning-oriented internal culture. They began sharing internal case studies where projects took months or years to succeed—spotlighting the human effort behind the algorithms.

Over time, this grounded approach allowed Airbus to realize tangible improvements in aircraft maintenance, supply chain prediction, and production optimization.[7]

Recognizing the Warning Signs

Airbus's experience is not unique. Many companies unintentionally fall into the Success Story Syndrome—a tendency to treat idealized AI case studies as blueprints, not inspiration.

The signs are subtle at first:

- Strategies are built around case studies, not internal audits.

- Expectations are set around fast, visible wins.

- Teams are unclear about how AI actually connects to their day-to-day work.

- Failures are avoided or quietly buried.

These signs don't just slow progress—they can quietly kill the momentum needed to build meaningful AI capacity.

Shifting the Narrative

To turn things around, Airbus made strategic adjustments. Instead of rushing to implement AI and advanced analytics with unrealistic expectations for quick results, they recalibrated their approach.

They focused first on addressing foundational issues—aligning their engineering and data science teams, resolving data inconsistencies, and establishing clear data governance. Airbus also invested heavily in change management, ensuring stakeholders were aligned and building a culture focused on continuous learning. They began documenting their challenges and successes, sharing case studies where projects took months or even years to bear fruit. These internal stories emphasized the human effort behind the technology, helping staff understand that AI is a complex, ongoing journey rather than a quick fix. Over time, this grounded approach led to real improvements in aircraft maintenance, supply chain forecasting, and production optimization.

The Learnings

The lesson here is simple but powerful: Don't let someone else's success story become your failure point.

If your organization is starting—or struggling—with AI adoption, consider these takeaways:

- Start with context, not comparisons. Tailor your approach to your data, your workflows, and your people.

- Redefine success. Look for steady improvements and learning moments, not instant wins.

- Talk about the messy middle. Normalize the friction and setbacks—it builds trust and resilience.

- Create your own stories. Internal case studies, even modest ones, are more useful than glossy external ones.

Even if your organization didn't meet its original AI goals, you could end up building something more valuable: a culture that was ready to keep learning, experimenting, and improving—with or without a perfect success story to point to.

YOUR PATH FORWARD: THE ADOPTION ACCELERATION FRAMEWORK

Success in overcoming AI resistance requires a systematic approach to implementation that builds acceptance through carefully planned phases. Begin with the foundation focus:

1. **Audit your current resistance landscape.** Start by understanding exactly where and why resistance exists in your organization.

2. **Identify quick-win opportunities.** Look for areas where AI can provide immediate, visible benefits. Michael's team found that automating routine paperwork was their perfect entry point. "Nothing builds trust quite like saving someone from their least favorite task," he noted.

3. **Create your champion network.** Identify and empower early adopters to help spread success stories.

BEYOND TEXT AND VOICE: THE RISE OF MULTIMODAL AI COACHING

AI coaching is no longer confined to text-based chatbots or voice assistants. The next generation of coaching systems will be multimodal, meaning they can process and respond to a combination of text, voice, video, facial expressions, body language, and even physiological signals.

For instance, researchers at MIT's Computer Science and Artificial Intelligence Laboratory are working on AI models that can analyze non-verbal cues, such as micro-expressions and shifts in posture, to assess engagement levels during conversations.[8] Imagine wearing smart glasses that provide real-time feedback on your presentation style, offering subtle corrections on everything from eye contact and hand gestures to vocal intonation and pacing.

Use Case:

- A salesperson giving a high-stakes pitch could receive real-time AI-driven insights via AR glasses, which highlight areas where they should slow down, increase enthusiasm, or make stronger eye contact with their audience.

- A job candidate could practice interview responses while AI evaluates their confidence based on vocal tone and posture, providing instant recommendations for improvement.

While these systems will offer invaluable coaching, we can only hope they deliver feedback with more diplomacy than a brutally honest friend—because nobody wants to hear that their power pose resembles a startled flamingo.

AI-POWERED BIORHYTHM OPTIMIZATION: PEAK PERFORMANCE, PERFECT TIMING

One of the most intriguing developments in AI coaching is its ability to optimize goal achievement by aligning tasks with biological rhythms. Studies show that humans have natural peak performance periods—some of us are morning warriors, while others hit their stride in the evening.

AI will soon automate and adapt scheduling based on our personal productivity patterns.

Researchers at the Stanford University Artificial Intelligence Laboratory are working on models that analyze sleep patterns, heart rate variability, and cognitive alertness to determine when a person is best suited for specific tasks.[9] AI coaching platforms of the future could integrate with wearable devices like the Oura Ring or Apple Watch to schedule negotiations, presentations, or brainstorming sessions at peak cognitive hours or adjust reminders and to-do lists dynamically based on energy levels and mental fatigue.

Of course, whether AI will convince the world to become morning people remains debatable—no amount of data-driven logic may sway the staunch defenders of the sacred snooze button. Ask my wife!

THE AGE OF AMBIENT INTELLIGENCE: COACHING THAT FADES INTO THE BACKGROUND

The next breakthrough in AI coaching involves "ambient intelligence," where AI works in the background without requiring active interaction. Imagine stepping into a conference room that automatically adjusts lighting, temperature, and soundscapes based on real-time AI analysis of your mood, speaking style, and audience engagement.

Companies like Amazon, Microsoft, and Google are already experimenting with smart environments that use AI-driven sensors to optimize workplace performance.[10] Future AI-powered "smart spaces" could adjust room lighting to subtly increase engagement when attention is dropping, modify air temperature based on cognitive load to enhance focus, or provide haptic feedback (gentle vibrations) to guide speech pacing or posture correction.

These smart spaces would transform interactions, making work environments more intuitive and responsive to human needs. However, we might need to set limits on AI's creativity, lest we find ourselves in boardrooms that suddenly transform into Zen meditation sanctuaries with whale sounds just because we looked a little stressed before a presentation.

THE AI COACHING REVOLUTION: A GLIMPSE INTO THE FUTURE

The landscape of AI coaching is transforming faster than a tech start-up's mission statement. Recent breakthroughs are opening doors we didn't even know existed, and the future holds even more promise.

AI coaching is evolving at an astonishing pace, driven by advancements in multimodal learning, ambient intelligence, and real-time performance augmentation. What once seemed like science fiction is now becoming reality, with AI systems poised to analyze, optimize, and even anticipate human behaviors in ways that were unimaginable just a few years ago.

SAY BYE TO SARAH AND MICHAEL

As we conclude our exploration of AI coaching, let's return to where we started: with Sarah and Michael. They have become proof of what's possible when you embrace the future of professional development.

Sarah's real estate team has evolved beyond her wildest expectations. As her digital dashboard shows her team's remarkable achievements, she looks to their biggest challenge: keeping up with all the ways her agents want to use AI coaching. Though she did have to put her foot down about using it to write poetry for property listings—even if that one sonnet about a walk-in closet was surprisingly moving.

Her team has achieved what once seemed impossible: an increase in property showings, improvement in client satisfaction, and higher closing rates. But perhaps most importantly, she now has a team that's excited about the future rather than fearful of it.

Michael's journey was equally transformative. From the loan officer who once stored all his knowledge in color-coded sticky notes, he's become a leader in AI-enhanced financial services. Though their improved numbers are remarkable, what really stands out is how AI coaching has transformed their entire approach to work.

SAY HI TO YOUR AI JOURNEY

The road to AI-enhanced excellence isn't about replacing human potential—it's about unleashing it in ways previously unimaginable. The journey begins with understanding where you are and envisioning where you want to go.

The most successful implementations start small but think big, focusing on quick wins that build momentum while laying the foundation for more ambitious transformations. The key lies in progressive mastery. Rather than attempting to revolutionize everything at once, successful organizations layer AI capabilities gradually. They might begin with basic process automation, then add data-driven insights, followed by predictive guidance, and finally, advanced optimization. This stepped approach allows teams to build confidence and competence while maintaining operational stability.

AI COACHING: THE NEW NORMAL

The AI coaching revolution is here, and it's moving beyond simple prompts and chat-based interactions into a world of immersive, real-time, and predictive guidance. The combination of multimodal AI, biorhythm-aware scheduling, and ambient intelligence will redefine how individuals and organizations unlock their full potential.

While we are still in the early stages of these advancements, the trajectory is clear: AI will become an invisible but indispensable coach, subtly shaping how we present, communicate, and perform at our peak. The question is no longer "Can AI help us improve?" but rather "How much will we allow AI to optimize our potential?"

And, of course, as long as AI remains helpful without critiquing our questionable dance moves at office parties, we're all for it.

THE FINAL EVOLUTION: FROM RESISTANCE TO RENAISSANCE

Remember, overcoming resistance to AI isn't about forcing adoption—it's about facilitating understanding. The goal isn't to make people love AI overnight—it's to help them see it as a partner in their success, even if it's a partner that occasionally needs a software update.

The most powerful moment in AI adoption isn't when people start using the technology—it's when they stop noticing they're using it.

The future of work isn't about choosing between human expertise and artificial intelligence—it's about creating that Synergy Effect where both work together to create possibilities that neither could achieve alone.

Your journey toward AI acceptance begins with a single step. As you embark on this path, remember that every major technological advancement in history faced initial resistance. Even electricity was once considered suspicious—and now we only panic when we can't find our phone chargers.

The key is to approach resistance not as an obstacle but as an opportunity for growth. After all, AI isn't going to take your job—it's going to help you be better at it.

"TELL THE CANDLE MAKERS, ELECTRICITY IS COMING"

The capabilities we've explored in this book are just the beginning. Multiple AI advancements promise to make AI coaching systems even more sophisticated. But perhaps the most exciting developments lie in areas we haven't yet imagined.

Your journey toward AI-enhanced excellence begins with a single step. Whether you're a solo entrepreneur like Michael or leading a growing team like Sarah, the principles remain the same: Embrace the future, trust the process, and keep pushing the boundaries of what's possible. And let AI be your coach.

Remember, every major transformation in history began with someone deciding to try something new.

The future is calling. It's time to answer.

Conclusion

Thanks for spending this journey with me. By now, you've seen that AI isn't about replacing us—it's about amplifying what we can do. The tools and strategies you've read about here are powerful, but like everything in tech, they're constantly evolving. Some tools may look different tomorrow, and a few may even disappear—that's the nature of innovation. What doesn't change is the mindset: staying curious, adaptable, and committed to learning.

That's why I created *The AI Coach* course. It's the most practical way to put all of this into action. Inside, I walk you through the top strategies and the latest tools step-by-step, so you don't just understand AI—you actually use it to grow your business and sharpen your skills. And because AI keeps moving fast, I update the course often with fresh insights and innovations, so you'll always stay ahead. As a thank-you for picking up this book, you can get $20 off with the code "AICoach20 "when you sign up at www.LetAIBeYourCoach.com.

Finally, I'd love to keep the conversation going. Connect with me on LinkedIn, share your thoughts, or leave a review on Amazon or any platform where you found this book. Your feedback means the world to me, and it helps more people discover how AI can truly become their coach. This isn't the end—it's just the beginning of your AI journey.

Acknowledgments

To the visionaries and entrepreneurs who are pushing the boundaries of what's possible with AI—thank you for inspiring me to think bigger and dream bolder. Your revolutionary work lit the path for this book.

To the countless teachers on YouTube, Coursera, webinars, and the many other learning platforms that became my classrooms—thank you for making the world of AI accessible to someone like me with no technical or software engineering background. Your generosity in teaching fueled this journey.

To my developers, who believed in the vision for my AI products long before it looked achievable—your conviction, creativity, and persistence made the impossible feel within reach.

And finally, to Puja Agarwal, my researcher and illustrator for this book—thank you for bringing clarity, depth, and visual storytelling to these pages. Your work elevated this project beyond what I could have imagined.

Essential AI Tools and Platforms

AI COACHING AND PROFESSIONAL DEVELOPMENT TOOLS

GPT-5 AND CLAUDE (LARGE LANGUAGE MODELS)

Best for: Day-to-day coaching, content creation, and problem-solving

Key features:

- Real-time writing assistance and editing
- Complex problem-solving support
- Code generation and debugging
- Sales email and communication enhancement
- Strategy development and refinement

Practical applications:

- Creating personalized client communications
- Developing marketing content
- Analyzing complex business scenarios

- Generating and refining presentations
- Role-playing sales conversations

GONG.IO

Best for: Sales coaching and conversation intelligence

Key features:

- Real-time call analysis
- Deal intelligence
- Performance benchmarking
- Customer interaction patterns
- Automated coaching recommendations

Practical applications:

- Analyzing sales calls for improvement opportunities
- Identifying successful conversation patterns
- Training new sales representatives
- Tracking deal progress and risk factors
- Enhancing customer interaction quality

MINDTICKLE

Best for: Sales readiness and skill development

Key features:

- Personalized learning paths
- Role-play scenarios
- Skill assessments
- Gamified learning experiences
- Performance analytics

MARKETING AND CONTENT CREATION TOOLS
JASPER.AI (FORMERLY JARVIS)

Best for: Advanced content creation and marketing

Key features:

- Long-form content generation
- Marketing copy creation
- Multi-language support
- Brand voice customization
- SEO suggestions

Practical applications:

- Creating blog posts and articles
- Generating social media content
- Writing email marketing campaigns
- Developing ad copy
- Crafting product descriptions

COPY.AI

Best for: Marketing copy and creative content

Key features:

- Digital ad copy generation
- Email sequence creation
- Product description writing
- Social media content creation
- Multiple tone and style options

Practical applications:

- Creating compelling headlines
- Generating marketing angles
- Writing engaging social posts
- Developing email newsletters
- Crafting website copy

SALES AND CUSTOMER SERVICE TOOLS
CHORUS.AI

Best for: Sales call analysis and coaching

Key features:

- Real-time conversation analysis
- Smart topic detection
- Sentiment analysis
- Coaching moments identification
- Performance trending

Practical applications:

- Training new sales representatives
- Improving customer interactions
- Identifying successful sales patterns
- Enhancing team collaboration
- Tracking performance metrics

HUBSPOT SALES HUB AI

Best for: Integrated sales and marketing

Key features:

- Predictive lead scoring
- Email sequence optimization
- Meeting scheduling automation
- Deal pipeline analytics
- Customer interaction tracking

Practical applications:

- Managing customer relationships
- Automating follow-ups
- Tracking deal progress
- Analyzing sales performance
- Optimizing outreach strategies

PERSONAL DEVELOPMENT AND LEARNING TOOLS
COURSERA AI-ENHANCED LEARNING

Best for: Professional skill development

Key features:

- Personalized learning paths
- AI-driven course recommendations
- Progress tracking
- Skill assessments
- Interactive exercises

Practical applications:

- Developing new skills
- Enhancing current capabilities

- Career advancement planning
- Knowledge verification
- Professional certification

LINKEDIN LEARNING WITH AI

Best for: Business skill development

Key features:
- Personalized course suggestions
- Skill path mapping
- Progress tracking
- Industry-specific learning tracks
- Integration with LinkedIn profile

Practical applications:
- Career development
- Skill enhancement
- Professional networking
- Industry knowledge acquisition
- Certification preparation

PROJECT MANAGEMENT AND PRODUCTIVITY TOOLS
ASANA WITH AI FEATURES

Best for: Project and team management

Key features:
- Task prioritization
- Workload optimization

- Timeline predictions
- Resource allocation
- Progress tracking

Practical applications:

- Managing team projects
- Optimizing workflows
- Resource planning
- Timeline management
- Performance tracking

MOTION

Best for: AI-powered time management

Key features:

- Intelligent scheduling
- Priority management
- Meeting optimization
- Focus time blocking
- Calendar analytics

Practical applications:

- Time management
- Meeting scheduling
- Task prioritization
- Productivity optimization
- Work-life balance management

IMPLEMENTATION AND INTEGRATION TOOLS
ZAPIER WITH AI

Best for: Workflow automation

Key features:

- Automated workflow creation
- AI-powered integration suggestions
- Error detection and correction
- Performance optimization
- Custom automation rules

Practical applications:

- Connecting different tools
- Automating repetitive tasks
- Streamlining workflows
- Data synchronization
- Process optimization

MICROSOFT POWER AUTOMATE

Best for: Enterprise automation

Key features:

- AI-powered workflow creation
- Document processing
- Process automation
- Integration capabilities
- Analytics and reporting

Practical applications:

- Business process automation
- Document handling
- System integration
- Workflow optimization
- Data processing

NOTE TO READERS

This list represents some of the leading tools available at the time of publication. The AI tool landscape evolves rapidly, so I recommended to always do the following:

- Research current pricing and features before making decisions.

- Start with free trials when available.

- Evaluate tools based on your specific needs.

- Consider scalability for future growth.

- Check for integration capabilities with your existing systems.

Master Implementation Framework

THE IMPLEMENTATION FRAMEWORK: A STEP-BY-STEP GUIDE

Tool: Use any large language model of your choice (e.g., ChatGPT, Gemini, or Claude).

SECTION 1: INITIAL ASSESSMENT AND PLANNING
Step 1: Current State Analysis

Purpose: Create a detailed analysis of your current organizational processes.

Prompt 1: Process Analysis

> I want to analyze my organization's current processes
> to identify areas where AI could help. My business is
> [describe your business]. Please help me create a struc-
> tured assessment by asking me relevant questions about
> our operations, one at a time. After gathering information,
> provide a summary of potential AI implementation areas.

Prompt 2: Pain Point Identification

> Based on these processes, [list main processes from previous response], help me identify our biggest operational challenges and inefficiencies. For each challenge:
>
> 1. Rate its impact on our business (1–10).
> 2. Suggest potential AI solutions.
> 3. Estimate implementation difficulty (easy/medium/hard).
>
> Please format this as a clear, prioritized list.

Step 2: Goal Setting

Purpose: Define clear, measurable AI implementation goals.

Prompt: Goal Development

> Help me develop SMART goals for implementing AI in my [specific area] process. Consider that I'm new to AI implementation. For each goal:
>
> 1. Make it specific and measurable.
> 2. Include a realistic time frame.
> 3. Suggest key performance indicators.
> 4. Include potential challenges to watch for.

SECTION 2: TEAM DEVELOPMENT AND COMMUNICATION
Step 3: Team Skills Assessment

Purpose: Create a skills inventory and identify training needs.

Prompt 1: Skills Analysis

> I need to assess my team's readiness for AI imple-
> mentation. Help me create a simple skills assessment
> questionnaire that covers:
> 1. Current technical skills
> 2. Experience with digital tools
> 3. Attitude toward technology
> 4. Learning preferences
> 5. Areas of interest in AI
>
> Format this as a survey that I can distribute to my team.

Prompt 2: Training Plan Development

> Based on these skill gaps [list main gaps identified], help
> me create a basic training plan for my team. Include:
> 1. Essential skills to develop first
> 2. Recommended learning resources (preferably free or
>   low-cost)
> 3. Timeline for skill development
> 4. Ways to measure progress
> 5. Practice exercises for each skill
>
> Present this as a step-by-step learning path suitable for
> beginners.

Step 4: Communication Planning

Prompt 1: Announcement Creation

Help me craft an announcement about implementing AI in our organization. Consider:

1. The team might be nervous about AI.
2. We want to emphasize human–AI collaboration.
3. We need to clearly explain the benefits.
4. We should address common concerns.
5. We want to maintain an optimistic but realistic tone.

Please write this in a clear, friendly style that would be appropriate for [describe your team culture].

Prompt 2: FAQ Development

Based on this announcement [paste announcement], help me create an FAQ document that:

1. Addresses common concerns about AI
2. Explains how daily work will change
3. Outlines the implementation timeline
4. Clarifies roles and responsibilities
5. Provides resources for learning more

Format this as a comprehensive but easy to read document, suitable for all skill levels.

SECTION 3: INITIAL IMPLEMENTATION
Step 5: Starting with Simple AI Tools

Prompt 1: Task Identification

> I want to start with a simple AI implementation. Here are our main daily tasks [list tasks]. Help me identify:
>
> 1. The easiest tasks to automate first
> 2. Specific AI tools for each task (free or low-cost options)
> 3. Step-by-step implementation instructions
> 4. Expected time savings
> 5. Potential challenges and solutions
>
> Focus on tasks that can show quick wins to build team confidence.

Prompt 2: Process Documentation

> Help me create a simple guide for using [specific AI tool] for [specific task]. Include:
>
> 1. Login and setup instructions
> 2. Basic commands or prompts to use
> 3. Best practices and tips
> 4. Common mistakes to avoid
> 5. Troubleshooting guide
>
> Write this for someone who has never used AI tools before.

SECTION 4: MEASURING SUCCESS
Step 6: Setting Up Basic Analytics

Prompt 1: Metrics Definition

Help me create a simple metrics-tracking system for our
AI implementation. We want to measure:

1. Time saved on tasks
2. Error reduction
3. Team adoption rates
4. Cost savings
5. Employee satisfaction

Please provide:

1. Specific metrics to track
2. How to measure each metric
3. Simple formulas for calculations
4. Suggested tracking frequency
5. Free or low-cost tools for tracking

Prompt 2: Progress Report Template

Help me create a weekly progress report template that
tracks our AI implementation. Include:

1. Key metrics summary
2. Wins and challenges
3. Team feedback highlights
4. Next steps
5. Resources needed

Make it simple enough for anyone to fill out in fifteen
minutes or less.

Step 7: Getting Team Feedback

Prompt 1: Feedback Survey Creation

> Help me create a user-friendly feedback form about our
> AI implementation. Include questions about:
> 1. Ease of use
> 2. Time savings
> 3. Challenges faced
> 4. Desired improvements
> 5. Support needed
>
> Make questions specific but not overwhelming. Include
> both rating scales and open-ended questions.

Prompt 2: Feedback Analysis

> Here is the feedback data from our team [paste data].
> Please help me:
> 1. Identify common themes
> 2. Spot urgent issues
> 3. Find improvement opportunities
> 4. Recognize successes
> 5. Prioritize next steps
>
> Present this in a clear format I can share with
> stakeholders.

SECTION 5: SCALING AND OPTIMIZATION
Step 8: Expanding AI Usage

Prompt 1: Expansion Planning

> Based on our success with [initial AI implementation], help me plan the next phase of AI adoption. Consider:
> 1. Which processes to automate next
> 2. Required resources
> 3. Potential challenges
> 4. Training needs
> 5. Timeline suggestions
>
> Provide a step-by-step expansion plan that builds on our current success.

Prompt 2: Advanced Use Cases

> For these processes [list successful AI implementations], help me identify:
> 1. Advanced features we might not be using
> 2. Integration opportunities with other tools
> 3. Automation possibilities
> 4. Efficiency improvements
> 5. New applications
>
> Focus on practical improvements we can implement with basic technical skills.

Step 9: Documentation and Best Practices

Prompt 1: Process Documentation

Help me create a comprehensive but user-friendly guide for our AI tools and processes. Include:

1. Step-by-step instructions
2. Best practices
3. Common troubleshooting
4. Tips and tricks
5. Resource links

Format this as an easy-to-update digital document that the team can easily reference.

Prompt 2: Training Material Creation

Based on our documented processes [paste key processes], help me create training materials for new team members. Include:

1. Getting started guide
2. Basic tutorials
3. Practice exercises
4. Assessment questions
5. Reference cheat sheets

Make these materials suitable for self-paced learning.

QUICK REFERENCE: PROMPT STARTERS

Use these basic prompts to get started with any AI task.

1. Analysis Prompt

> I need to analyze [specific task/process]. Please help me by:
> 1. Breaking it down into steps
> 2. Identifying improvement opportunities
> 3. Suggesting AI tools
> 4. Estimating potential benefits
> 5. Highlighting possible challenges

2. Problem-Solving Prompt

> I'm facing this challenge: [Describe problem]. Please help me:
> 1. Understand the root cause
> 2. Generate possible solutions
> 3. Evaluate each option
> 4. Create an action plan
> 5. Identify success metrics

3. Improvement Prompt

> We want to improve our [specific process]. Please help me:
> 1. Assess current state
> 2. Identify inefficiencies
> 3. Suggest AI solutions
> 4. Create implementation steps
> 5. Define success criteria

Remember:

- Start with simpler prompts and gradually increase complexity.

- Be specific about your needs and context.

- Iterate on prompts based on the responses.

- Save successful prompts for future use.

- Share effective prompts with your team.

Notes

CHAPTER 1

1. Stitch Fix, "How We're Revolutionizing Personal Styling with Generative AI,"
    Stitch Fix Newsroom, June 29, 2023, https://newsroom.stitchfix.com/blog/
    how-were-revolutionizing-personal-styling-with-generative-ai/.

2. "AI Case Study: UPS Saves over 10 Million Gallons of Fuel and up to $400M in Costs
    Annually with Advanced Telematics and Analysis," Best Practice AI, https://www.
    bestpractice.ai/ai-case-study-best-practice/ups_saves_over_10_million_gallons_of_fuel_
    and_up_to_%24400m_in_costs_annually_with_advanced_telematics_and_analysis.

3. Richelle Deveau, Sonia Joseph Griffin, and Steve Reis, "AI-Powered Marketing and
    Sales Reach New Heights with Generative AI," McKinsey & Company, May 11, 2023,
    https://www.mckinsey.com/capabilities/growth-marketing-and-sales/our-insights/
    ai-powered-marketing-and-sales-reach-new-heights-with-generative-ai.

4. GW Prime, "The Story of Coca-Cola and Its AI-Powered Vending Machines,"
    Geospatial World, https://geospatialworld.net/prime/case-study/
    the-story-of-coca-cola-and-its-ai-powered-vending-machines/.

CHAPTER 2

1. Viktor Laufs, "Millions in Lost Productivity: The Hidden Cost of 9+ Hours of
    Weekly Search Time," LinkedIn, March 13, 2025, https://www.linkedin.com/pulse/
    millions-lost-productivity-hidden-cost-9-hours-weekly-viktor-laufs-e9c2c/.

2. IBM, "Expert Service, 60% Faster," October 2023, https://www.ibm.com/case-studies/
    credit-mutuel.

3. Nathan Van Zyl, "7 Ways HubSpot CRM Can Improve Your Customer Acquisition,"
    Uku Inbound, November 20, 2021, https://grow.ukuinbound.com/blog/
    7-ways-hubspot-crm-can-improve-your-customer-acquisition.

4. Chetan Sharma and Jan Overgoor, "Scaling Knowledge at Airbnb," Medium, February 25, 2016, https://medium.com/airbnb-engineering/scaling-knowledge-at-airbnb-875d73eff091.

5. Matt Saunders, "Spotify Reveals Metrics for Success of Developer Portal Backstage," InfoQ, April 24, 2023, https://www.infoq.com/news/2023/04/spotify-success-backstage; Meg Watson, "How Spotify Measures the Value of Backstage," Spotify, March 30, 2023, https://backstage.spotify.com/discover/blog/how-spotify-measures-backstage-roi/; Helen Greul, "How We Measure Backstage Success at Spotify," Spotify, October 18, 2021, https://backstage.spotify.com/discover/blog/measuring-backstage-success-at-spotify.

6. "The Definition of Knowledge Sharing—Just What Is It?" Document360, February 6, 2024, https://document360.com/blog/definition-of-knowledge-sharing/.

7. Institute for Collaborative Working (ICW), "Has your organisation realised the full potential of collaborative working? A company's collaboration index increases sales by 27% and improves customer satisfaction ratings by 41%, according to data from Frost & Sullivan. The study also showed that collaboration improves product quality by 34% and improves product development by 30%. To learn more about the benefits of collaboration, explore this report: https://lnkd.in/eNkK6hkX #collaboriveworking #collaboration," LinkedIn, 2023, https://www.linkedin.com/posts/institute-for-collaborative-working_collaboriveworking-collaboration-activity-6990973684517584896-qhUW/?trk=public_profile_like_view.

8. Josh Blatt, "U.S. Should Build Capacity to Rapidly Detect and Respond to AI Developments; New Report Identifies Workforce Challenges and Opportunities," news release, National Academies, November 21, 2024, https://www.nationalacademies.org/news/u-s-should-build-capacity-to-rapidly-detect-and-respond-to-ai-developments-new-report-identifies-workforce-challenges-and-opportunities.

9. Michelle Vaccaro, Abdullah Almaatouq, and Thomas Malone, "When Combinations of Humans and AI Are Useful: A Systematic Review and Meta-Analysis," *Nature Human Behaviour* 8 (2024): 2293–303, https://www.nature.com/articles/s41562-024-02024-1.

CHAPTER 3

1. Jason Kellington, "Elevating Internal Communications at Microsoft with AI," Microsoft, January 23, 2025, https://www.microsoft.com/insidetrack/blog/elevating-internal-communications-at-microsoft-with-ai/.

2. Jitesh Nair and Balaswamy Pasala, *Unilever's AI-Powered Internal Talent Marketplace Unlocks Workforce Capacity*, IBS Center for Management Research, 2021, https://www.thecasecentre.org/products/view?id=175665; Mark McGraw, "Unilever's Internal

Talent Marketplace: Putting Skills on Display," i4cp, December 17, 2019, https://www.i4cp.com/productivity-blog/putting-skills-on-display-in-unilevers-internal-talent-marketplace; Maya Finkelstein, "Unilever, the Consumer Goods Giant, Implements AI to Retain, Develop, and Engage Talent," Gloat, June 24, 2019, https://gloat.com/blog/unilever-ai-retain-develop-engage-talent-innermobility-gloat/.

3. Meredith Somers, "How Generative AI Can Boost Highly Skilled Workers' Productivity," MIT Sloan School of Management, October 19, 2023, https://mitsloan.mit.edu/ideas-made-to-matter/how-generative-ai-can-boost-highly-skilled-workers-productivity.

4. Domino's Pizza, "Domino's on Quest for Digital Dominance Using Artificial Intelligence," PR Newswire, April 23, 2018, https://www.prnewswire.com/news-releases/dominos-on-quest-for-digital-dominance-using-artificial-intelligence-300633827.html.

5. Eric Hazen et al., *A New Future of Work: The Race to Deploy AI and Raise Skills in Europe and Beyond* (McKinsey & Company, 2024).

6. Fabrizio Dell'Acqua et al., "Navigating the Jagged Technological Frontier: Field Experimental Evidence of the Effects of AI on Knowledge Worker Productivity and Quality," Harvard Business School working paper, 2023, https://www.hbs.edu/faculty/Pages/item.aspx?num=64700.

CHAPTER 4

1. Tenika Small and Katie Nguyen, "Introducing Dropbox Dash for Business—AI-Powered Universal Search That Finds Anything and Protects Everything at Work," news release, Dropbox, October 15, 2024, https://investors.dropbox.com/news-releases/news-release-details/introducing-dropbox-dash-business-ai-powered-universal-search.

2. Joe Barron, "AI for Sales Prospecting: The Ultimate Guide," Cognism, August 26, 2025, https://www.cognism.com/blog/ai-sales-prospecting.

3. "Lead Scoring Software," HubSpot, https://www.hubspot.com/products/marketing/lead-scoring.

4. Karan Nigam, "Accelerating Sales with Unified Data in the AI Era," Microsoft, February 3, 2025, https://www.microsoft.com/en-us/dynamics-365/blog/business-leader/2025/02/03/accelerating-sales-with-unified-data-in-the-ai-era/.

5. "How Heatmap Analytics Helps You Find Out What People Actually Do on Your Website," Hotjar, https://www.hotjar.com/heatmap-analytics/.

6. "Configure Predictive Lead Scoring," Microsoft, August 7, 2025, https://learn.microsoft.com/en-us/dynamics365/sales/configure-predictive-lead-scoring.

7. "100+ AI Statistics Shaping Business in 2025," Vena Solutions, May 7, 2025, https://www.venasolutions.com/blog/ai-statistics.

8. "Real-Time Customer Profile Overview," Adobe, April 1, 2025, https://experienceleague. adobe.com/en/docs/experience-platform/profile/home.

9. "Analytics," Hootsuite, https://www.hootsuite.com/platform/analytics; "Social Media Inbox Management," Hootsuite, https://www.hootsuite.com/platform/ social-media-inbox.

10. Jeffrey Dastin, "Insight - Amazon Scraps Secret AI Recruiting Tool That Showed Bias Against Women," Reuters, October 10, 2018, https://www.reuters.com/article/world/ insight-amazon-scraps-secret-ai-recruiting-tool-that-showed-bias-against-women- idUSKCN1MK0AG/.

11. Kashmir Hill, "How Target Figured Out a Teen Girl Was Pregnant Before Her Father Did," *Forbes*, February 16, 2012, https://www.forbes.com/sites/kashmirhill/2012/02/16/ how-target-figured-out-a-teen-girl-was-pregnant-before-her-father-did.

12. Bernard Marr, "Why Apple Intelligence Sets a New Gold Standard for AI Privacy," *Forbes*, September 11, 2024, https://www.forbes.com/sites/bernardmarr/2024/09/11/ why-apple-intelligence-sets-a-new-gold-standard-for-ai-privacy/.

13. "Differential Privacy," Apple, https://www.apple.com/privacy/docs/ Differential_Privacy_Overview.pdf.

14. "Responsible AI," IBM, https://www.ibm.com/trust/responsible-ai.

CHAPTER 5

1. Yoodli, "How Korn Ferry Transformed Their Coaching Offering Using Yoodli AI Communication Coach," October 28, 2024, https://yoodli.ai/our-partnerships/ how-korn-ferry-transformed-their-client-coaching-offering-using-yoodli-ai.

2. Korn Ferry, "Korn Ferry and Yoodli Partner to Bring AI-powered Communication Coaching to Organizations Worldwide," news release, December 20, 2023, https://www.kornferry.com/about-us/press/korn-ferry-and-yoodli-partner-to- bring-ai-powered-communication-coaching.

3. Yoodli, "How Korn Ferry Transformed Their Coaching Offering."

4. Gavin Lockitch, "The Power of 'Micro-Moments' in Leadership and Business: Small Shifts, Massive Impact," LinkedIn, May 7, 2025, https://www.linkedin.com/pulse/ power-micro-moments-leadership-business-small-shifts-massive-gavin-wi0vf/.

5. Laura Fres, "The Power of Micro-Moments in Product Marketing," Product Marketing Alliance, June 3, 2024, https://www.productmarketingalliance.com/ micro-moments-in-product-marketing/.

6. Saul McLeod, "Zone Of Proximal Development," Simply Psychology, October 16, 2025, https://www.simplypsychology.org/zone-of-proximal-development.html.

7. Jose Carranza, "Ergeon - Success Story with SellMeThisPen AI," SellMeThisPen, March 5, 2024, https://www.sellmethispen.ai/blog/ergeon-success-story-with-sellmethispen-ai.

CHAPTER 6

1. "Case Studies in AI-Driven Lead Targeting: Success Stories and Lessons Learned from B2B Sales Teams in 2025," SuperAGI, June 28, 2025, https://superagi.com/case-studies-in-ai-driven-lead-targeting-success-stories-and-lessons-learned-from-b2b-sales-teams-in-2025/.

2. Phil Britt, "5 AI Case Studies in Sales," VKTR, March 2, 2024, https://www.vktr.com/ai-disruption/5-ai-case-studies-in-sales/.

3. Sudarshan Lamkhede and Christoph Kofler, "Recommendations and Results Organization in Netflix Search," Netflix, September 13, 2021, https://research.netflix.com/publication/recommendations-and-results-organization-in-netflix-search.

4. Busines NewsWire, "How Walmart's AI-Driven Inventory Management Enhances Forecast Accuracy and Reduces Stockouts," Big News Network, August 18, 2025, https://www.bignewsnetwork.com/news/278515680/how-walmart-ai-driven-inventory-management-enhances-forecast-accuracy-and-reduces-stockouts.

5. "5 Ways Sephora Is Using AI [Case Study] [2025]," DigitalDefynd, https://digitaldefynd.com/IQ/sephora-using-ai-case-study/.

6. "Using AI in CRM: Top AI-Powered CRM Platforms," Shopify, May 6, 2025, https://www.shopify.com/in/blog/ai-in-crm.

7. "Upwork's RevOps Team Rockets to 95% Sales Forecast Accuracy Using Gong," Gong, https://www.gong.io/case-studies/upworks-revops-team-rockets-to-95-sales-forecast-accuracy-using-gong/.

8. "State of the Connected Customer Report," Salesforce, 2022, https://www.salesforce.com/eu/resources/research-reports/state-of-the-connected-customer-2022/.

9. Jochen Böringer et al., "Insights to Impact: Creating and Sustaining Data-Driven Commerical Growth," McKinsey & Company, January 18, 2022, https://www.mckinsey.com/capabilities/growth-marketing-and-sales/our-insights/insights-to-impact-creating-and-sustaining-data-driven-commercial-growth.

10. Nicolas de Bellefonds et al., *Where's the Value in AI* (Boston Consulting Group, 2024), https://media-publications.bcg.com/BCG-Wheres-the-Value-in-AI.pdf.

CHAPTER 7

1. Jordan Turner, "AI Presentation Design Trends for 2025," beautiful.ai, March 3, 2025, https://www.beautiful.ai/blog/ai-presentation-design-trends-for-2025.

2. "Paciolan Uses Beautiful.ai for the 'Wow' Factor," beautiful.ai, https://www.beautiful.ai/customers/paciolan.

3. Dustin Blank, "Arianna Huffington Uses ElevenLabs to Refresh Thrive for Its 10th Anniversary," ElevenLabs, February 3, 2025, https://elevenlabs.io/blog/arianna-huffington-uses-elevenlabs-to-refresh-thrive-for-its-10th-anniversary.

4. "Create a Replica of Your Voice That Sounds Just Like You," ElevenLabs. https://elevenlabs.io/voice-cloning.

5. Avi, "Create Your First Digital Twin with Avatar IV!" HeyGen, https://help.heygen.com/en/articles/12089286-create-your-first-digital-twin-with-avatar-iv.

6. "How Trivago Used HeyGen to Simultaneously Localize TV Ads in 30 Markets," HeyGen, https://www.heygen.com/customer-stories/trivago.

CHAPTER 8

1. "PRESS Healthfoods: Boosting Sales Using Meta Advantage+ Creative with Generative AI Features," Facebook, https://en-gb.facebook.com/business/success/press-healthfoods.

2. "Draivi Media Oy: Driving Loan and Credit Card Application Registrations with Meta Video and Photo Ads," Facebook, https://business.facebook.com/business/success/draivi-media-oy.

3. *Adobe 2025 AI and Digital Trends Report* (Adobe, 2025), https://business.adobe.com/resources/digital-trends-report.html.

4. *Microsoft 2024 Annual Report* (Microsoft Corporation, 2024), https://www.microsoft.com/investor/reports/ar24/.

5. Milana Saric, "How Brands Can Still Win Over Customers as Attention Spans Decrease on Social," Adweek, November 21, 2017, https://www.adweek.com/brand-marketing/how-brands-can-still-win-over-customers-as-attention-spans-decrease-on-social/.

6. "The Story of Coca-Cola and Its AI-Powered Vending Machines," Geospatial World, https://geospatialworld.net/prime/case-study/the-story-of-coca-cola-and-its-ai-powered-vending-machines/.

7. Sharma and Overgoor, "Scaling Knowledge at Airbnb."

8. Harrison Schell, "Visualizing the Daily Scroll of the Average Social Media User," Visual Capitalist, February 1, 2025, https://www.visualcapitalist.com/cp/visualizing-the-daily-scroll-of-the-average-social-media-user/.

9. Kate Moran, "How People Read Online: New and Old Findings," Nielsen Norman Group, April 5, 2020, https://www.nngroup.com/articles/how-people-read-online/.

10. "Spotify Used Your Data For Marketing," Marketing Maverick, January 30, 2025, https://marketingmaverick.io/p/thanks-2016-it-s-been-weird-billboard-campaign-by-spotify.

11. "How Mailchimp's Misinterpretation Meme Built Brand Affinity," WARC, December 20, 2017, https://www.warc.com/newsandopinion/news/how-mailchimps-misinterpretation-meme-built-brand-affinity/en-gb/39777.

12. Rohan S., "What if your customers became your best marketers without you paying them a single dollar? Apple cracked this code with their "Shot on iPhone" campaign—and the results are staggering," LinkedIn, September 2025, https://www.linkedin.com/posts/iamdigisolution_shotoniphone-activity-7360521007800942592-vRw9/.

13. Mike Gunderson, "'How to Create Advertising that Sells' by David Ogilvy," Gundir, https://gundir.com/resource/how-to-create-advertising-that-sells-by-david-ogilvy/.

14. Ashok Chandrashekar et al., "Artwork Personalization at Netflix," *Netflix Technology Blog*, December 7, 2017, https://netflixtechblog.com/artwork-personalization-c589f074ad76.

15. Facebook IQ, "Capturing Attention in Feed: The Science Behind Effective Video Creative. Facebook Business," Meta, April 20, 2016, https://www.facebook.com/business/news/insights/capturing-attention-feed-video-creative.

16. Liza Colburn, "Generative AI and Personalization: How to Increase ROI," Persado, January 13, 2023, https://www.persado.com/articles/generative-ai-and-personalization/.

17. "How eBay Pioneered the Use of Brand Language Optimization and Paved the Way for Marketers Everywhere," HubSpot, https://f.hubspotusercontent20.net/hubfs/4094824/ebay_CaseStudy_Updated.pdf

18. *Marketing & Sales: Big Data, Analytics, and the Future of Marketing & Sales* (McKinsey & Company, March 2015), https://www.mckinsey.com/~/media/mckinsey/business%20functions/marketing%20and%20sales/our%20insights/ebook%20big%20data%20analytics%20and%20the%20future%20of%20marketing%20sales/big-data-ebook.pdf.

19. Mike Wheatley, "Netflix Dominates Video Streaming with Highest Subscription, Retention Rates," HDTVtest, December 11, 2018, https://www.hdtvtest.co.uk/news/Netflix-Dominates-Video-Streaming-with-Highest-Subscription-Retention-Rates.

20. "How Adidas Increased AOV by 259% and Revenue Per User by 18.5% in One Month with Insider," Insider, https://useinsider.com/case-studies/adidas/.

21. "Adidas Taps into Commerce Growth to Expand New Customer Base," Adidas, https://www.criteo.com/success-stories/adidas/.

CHAPTER 9

1. "New Epsilon Research Indicates 80% of Consumers Are More Likely to Make a Purchase When Brands Offer Personalized Experiences," Epsilon, January 9, 2018, https://www.epsilon.com/us/about-us/pressroom/new-epsilon-research-indicates-80-of-consumers-are-more-likely-to-make-a-purchase-when-brands-offer-personalized-experiences.

2. *2023 Digital Trends* (Adobe, 2023), https://business.adobe.com/content/dam/cct/creativecloud/business/teams/whitepapers/pdf/Adobe-Digital-Trends-2023.pdf; Kevin Lindsay, "Personalization at Scale at the Intersection of Marketing and Consumer Journeys," *Adobe for Business* (blog), March 26, 2024, https://business.adobe.com/blog/the-latest/personalization-at-scale-at-the-intersection-of-marketing-and-consumer-journeys.

3. "Synchrony Increases Credit Card Applications with Personalization," Dynamic Yield, https://www.dynamicyield.com/case-studies/financial-services/.

4. Christine Lockhart-Morse, "$42 to $1 ROI with eMail Marketing," LinkedIn, February 28, 2024, https://www.linkedin.com/pulse/42-1-roi-email-marketing-christine-morse-vazle/.

5. "AI Product Recommendations: How They Work and Drive Sales," VisionX, January 1, 2025, https://visionx.io/blog/product-recommendation-with-ai/.

6. Ian MacKenzie, Chris Meyer, and Steve Noble, "How Retailers Can Keep up with Consumers," McKinsey & Company, October 1, 2013, https://www.mckinsey.com/industries/retail/our-insights/how-retailers-can-keep-up-with-consumers.

7. "Marks & Spencer Leverages AI to Drive Hundreds of Millions in Revenue with Personalization Program," Persado, 2022, https://www.persado.com/wp-content/uploads/2024/07/Marks-and-Spencer-leverages-AI-to-drive-hundreds-of-millions-in-revenue-with-personalisation-program2.pdf.

8. "Conversational AI Marketing Trends Report," Salesloft, January 16, 2024, https://www.salesloft.com/resources/guides/conversational-ai-marketing-trends-report; PR Newswire, "Drift Defines Future of Conversational Marketing with New AI-Powered Innovations," Drift, October 3, 2023, https://www.prnewswire.com/news-releases/drift-defines-future-of-conversational-marketing-with-new-ai-powered-innovations-301945215.html.

9. Facebook IQ, "Capturing Attention in Feed."

10. Robert Lee, "LinkedIn Advertising Statistics 2025: Reach, Engagement, and Conversion Benchmarks," SQ Magazine, October 2, 2025, https://sqmagazine.co.uk/linkedin-advertising-statistics/.

11. Ivana Kotorcheviki, "Deep Brew: Transforming Starbucks into AI & Data-Driven Company," Hyperight, June 30, 2021, https://hyperight.com/deep-brew-transforming-starbucks-into-a-data-driven-company/.

12. Kotorcheviki, "Deep Brew"; Dany Kitishian, "Starbucks' AI Strategy: Analysis Of Dominance In Coffee," Klover.ai, July 23, 2025, https://www.klover.ai/starbucks-ai-strategy-analysis-of-dominance-in-coffee/; Amanda Greenwood, "How Starbucks Uses AI to Make a 30% ROI," The AI Report, April 11, 2024, https://www.theaireport.ai/articles/how-starbucks-uses-ai-to-make-a-30-roi.

CHAPTER 10

1. "Employee Training Statistics & Data in the U.S. (2024/2025)," HIGH5 Test, September 8, 2025, https://high5test.com/employee-training-statistics/; *The State of Organizations 2023* (McKinsey & Company, 2023), https://www.mckinsey.com/~/media/mckinsey/business%20functions/people%20and%20organizational%20performance/our%20insights/the%20state%20of%20organizations%202023/the-state-of-organizations-2023.pdf.

2. Athena Marousis, "What Is the Ebbinghaus Forgetting Curve? Examples and Strategies for Overcoming It," TalentCards blog, March 30, 2023, https://www.talentcards.com/blog/ebbinghaus-forgetting-curve/.

3. Michael Chui et al., "The State of AI in 2023: Generative AI's Breakout Year," McKinsey & Company, August 1, 2023, https://www.mckinsey.com/capabilities/quantumblack/our-insights/the-state-of-ai-in-2023-generative-ais-breakout-year.

4. Alexis Patterson, "Emotional Intelligence in Science: Pathway to Improving Equitable Groupwork and Enhancing Engagement in Scientific Practices?" (dissertation, Stanford University, May 2015), https://stacks.stanford.edu/file/druid:tw507sb9997/Patterson%20Final%20Dissertation-augmented.pdf.

5. Marousis, "What Is the Ebbinghaus."

6. Nicky Terblanche et al., "Comparing Artificial Intelligence and Human Coaching Goal Attainment Efficacy," *PLOS One* 17, no. 6 (June 21, 2022), https://pubmed.ncbi.nlm.nih.gov/35727801/.

7. Fabian Billing et al., "Building Workforce Skills at Scale to Thrive During—and After—the COVID-19 Crisis," McKinsey & Company, April 30, 2021, https://www.mckinsey.com/capabilities/people-and-organizational-performance/our-insights/building-workforce-skills-at-scale-to-thrive-during-and-after-the-covid-19-crisis.

8. Sagar Goel, Shubhankar Sohoni, and Lisa Krayer, "How GenAI Could Transform Learning and Development," *Harvard Business Review*, September 23, 2025, https://hbr.org/2025/09/how-gen-ai-could-transform-learning-and-development.

9.   MIT Sloan Office of Communication, "Humans and AI: Do They Work Better Together or Alone?" MIT Sloan School of Management, October 28, 2024, https://mitsloan.mit.edu/press/humans-and-ai-do-they-work-better-together-or-alone.

10. Tim Paradis, "AI Will Reshape the Global Labor Force. Employers Will Need to Help Their Workers Keep Up," *Business Insider*, August 28, 2024, https://www.businessinsider.com/ai-will-change-most-jobs-employers-help-workers-keep-up-2024-8.

CHAPTER 11

1.   Amy Edmondson and Olivia Jung, "The Turnaround at Ford Motor Company," Harvard Business School, revised August 2024, https://www.hbs.edu/faculty/Pages/item.aspx?num=59955; MoneyWatch, "Ford Posts $12.7B Loss in 2006, Worst Ever," news release, January 25, 2007, https://www.cbsnews.com/news/ford-posts-127b-loss-in-2006-worst-ever/.

2.   The Coca-Cola Company, "Coca-Cola Releases 2014/2015 Sustainability Report," press release, July 28, 2015, https://investors.coca-colacompany.com/news-events/press-releases/detail/776/coca-cola-releases-20142015-sustainability-report; "Sustainability," The Coca-Cola Company, https://www.coca-colacompany.com/about-us/sustainability.

3.   Stacia Garr and Andrew Liakopoulos, "Performance Management Is Broken," Deloitte, March 5, 2014, https://www.deloitte.com/us/en/insights/topics/talent/human-capital-trends/2014/hc-trends-2014-performance-management.html.

4.   Shannon Poynton et al., *2024 Global Human Capital Trends* (Deloitte Insights, 2024), https://www.deloitte.com/content/dam/insights/articles/2024/glob176836_global-human-capital-trends-2024/DI_Global-Human-Capital-Trends-2024.pdf.

5.   Chui et al., "The State of AI in 2023."

6.   Nigel Guenole and Sheri Feinzig, "The Business Case for AI in HR," IBM Watson Talent, November 2018, https://forms.workday.com/content/dam/web/en-us/documents/case-studies/ibm-business-case-ai-in-hr.pdf; Fei Qin and Thomas Kochan, "The Learning System at IBM: A Case Study," MIT Sloan School of Management, December 3, 2020, https://mitsloan.mit.edu/sites/default/files/2022-06/Qin%20and%20Kochan%20The%20Learning%20System%20at%20IBM%2012%202020.pdf; David Kiron and Barbara Spindel, "Rebooting Work for a Digital Era," *MIT Sloan Management Review*, February 19, 2019, https://sloanreview.mit.edu/case-study/rebooting-work-for-a-digital-era/.

7.   Elliott Choi, Maxime Voisin, and Ana Cismaru, "Notion Helps Cohere Save 7+ Hours per Week for Faster Shipping Velocity," Notion, https://www.notion.com/customers/cohere.

CHAPTER 12

1. John McCarthy, "History of Lisp," Stanford University, February 12, 1979, http://jmc.stanford.edu/articles/lisp/lisp.pdf; *Stanford Institute for Human-Centered Artificial Intelligence*, annual report (Stanford University, 2024), https://hai-production.s3.amazonaws.com/files/2025-02/2024-hai-annual-report-02252025-digital.pdf.

2. Michael Woolridge and Nicholas Jennings, "Intelligent Agents: Theory and Practice," *Knowledge Engineering Review* (October 1994) https://www.cs.cmu.edu/~motionplanning/papers/sbp_papers/integrated1/woodridge_intelligent_agents.pdf.

3. "75 Years of Innovation: CALO (Cognitive Assistant that Learns and Organizes)," SRI, http://sri.com/75-years-of-innovation/75-years-of-innovation-calo-cognitive-assistant-that-learns-and-organizes/; Nigel Shadbolt, Wendy Hall, and Tim Berners-Lee, "The Semantic Web Revisited," *IEEE Intelligent Systems* 21, no. 3 (May/June 2006), https://eprints.soton.ac.uk/262614/1/Semantic_Web_Revisted.pdf.

4. Ashish Vaswani et al., "Attention Is All You Need," (31st Conference on Neural Information Processing Systems (NIPS 2017), Long Beach, California, December 4–9, 2017, https://proceedings.neurips.cc/paper_files/paper/2017/file/3f5ee243547dee91fbd053c1c4a845aa-Paper.pdf); Jakob Uszkoreit, "Transformer: A Novel Neural Network Architecture for Language Understanding," Google Research blog, August 31, 2017, https://research.google/blog/transformer-a-novel-neural-network-architecture-for-language-understanding/.

5. Stanford Institute for Human-Centered Artificial Intelligence; Stanford University, "AI Agents Simulate 1,052 Individuals' Personalities with Impressive Accuracy," news release, January 21, 2025, https://hai.stanford.edu/news/ai-agents-simulate-1052-individuals-personalities-with-impressive-accuracy.

6. OpenAI, "Introducing ChatGPT Agent: Bridging Research and Action," news release, July 17, 2025, https://openai.com/index/introducing-chatgpt-agent/.

7. OpenAI, "Introducing ChatGPT."

8. "Introducing Computer Use, a New Claude 3.5 Sonnet, and Claude 3.5 Haiku," Anthropic, October 22, 2024, https://www.anthropic.com/news/3-5-models-and-computer-use.

9. "How We Built Our Multi-Agent Research System," Anthropic, June 13, 2025, https://www.anthropic.com/engineering/multi-agent-research-system.

10. OpenAI, "Introducing ChatGPT."

11. "Our Framework for Developing Safe and Trustworthy Agents," Anthropic, August 4, 2025, https://www.anthropic.com/news/our-framework-for-developing-safe-and-trustworthy-agents.

12. OpenAI, "Introducing ChatGPT."

13. National Academies of Sciences, Engineering, and Medicine, "U.S. Should Build Capacity to Rapidly Detect and Respond to AI Developments: New Report Identifies Workforce Challenges and Opportunities," news release, November 21, 2024, https://www.nationalacademies.org/news/2024/11/u-s-should-build-capacity-to-rapidly-detect-and-respond-to-ai-developments-new-report-identifies-workforce-challenges-and-opportunities.

CHAPTER 13

1. World Economic Forum, *Future of Jobs Report* (WEF Publications, 2024), https://medium.com/@knocksfuture/world-economic-forum-future-of-jobs-report-2024-2d9be79281b3.

2. Jason Lange and Alexandra Alper, "Americans Fear AI Permanently Displacing Workers, Reuters/Ipsos Poll Finds," Reuters, August 20, 2025, https://www.reuters.com/world/us/americans-fear-ai-permanently-displacing-workers-reutersipsos-poll-finds-2025-08-19/.

3. World Economic Forum, *Future of Jobs Report*.

4. Salesforce, "AI Urgency Is Up but U.S. Adoption Is Slowing, Says New Slack Workforce Index," news release, November 12, 2024, https://www.salesforce.com/news/stories/ai-adoption-slows-statistics/.

5. Michael Mankins and Eric Garton, "How Spotify Balances Employee Autonomy and Accountability," Bain & Company, February 2017, https://www.bain.com/insights/how-spotify-balances-employee-autonomy-and-accountability-hbr/.

6. "Coursera Coach: Leveraging GenAI to Empower Learners," Coursera, June 5, 2024, https://blog.coursera.org/coursera-coach-leveraging-genai-to-empower-learners/.

7. Airbus, "Airbus Launches Skywise—Aviation's Open Data Platform," press release, June 20, 2017, https://www.airbus.com/en/newsroom/press-releases/2017-06-airbus-launches-skywise-aviations-open-data-platform.

8. "Towards Socially-Intelligent Nonverbal Foundation Models," MIT Media Lab, https://www.media.mit.edu/projects/nonverbal-social-intelligence/overview/.

9. "Bio: Andrea Goldstein-Piekarski," Stanford University, https://profiles.stanford.edu/andrea-goldstein-piekarski; "CoPsyN Sleep Lab," Stanford Medicine, https://med.stanford.edu/copsynsleeplab.html.

10. "35 Leading Smart Office Companies Shaping the Intelligent Workplace Market Through 2030," Research and Markets, https://www.researchandmarkets.com/articles/key-companies-in-smart-office; "Google Workspace Predictions for 2025: How Businesses Can Stay Ahead and Leverage Its Potential," Gear Cloud, December 9, 2024, https://gearcs.com/google-workspace-predictions-for-2025-how-businesses-can-stay-ahead-and-leverage-its-potential/.s

About the Author

SHASHANK SHEKHAR is the founder and CEO of InstaMortgage and InstaAI. Shashank has won the Stevie Award for Entrepreneur of the Year for four consecutive years. His writing has been published in *Forbes, Inc., Entrepreneur, HousingWire*, and *HuffPost*.

Shashank is a sought-after speaker and podcast guest. As a technologist, Shashank created "Rachel," the mortgage industry's first conversational AI digital human, and "InstaAI," a first-of-its-kind generative AI platform for loan officers. He published the first GPT by a mortgage company on the GPT store.

His last two books, *My First Home* and *Real Estate Unleashed*, were Amazon bestsellers.